PROPERTY OF
BAKER COLLEGE
Owosso Campus

MICHIGAN BEYOND 2000

by

William B. Johnston
Jane Newitt
David Reed

UNIVERSITY
PRESS OF
AMERICA

Lanham • New York • London

HUDSON
I·N·S·T·I·T·U·T·E

Copyright ©1987 by

Hudson Institute

University Press of America,® Inc.

4720 Boston Way
Lanham, MD 20706

3 Henrietta Street
London WC2E 8LU England

All rights reserved

Printed in the United States of America

British Cataloging in Publication Information Available

Library of Congress Cataloging-in-Publication Data

Hudson Institute.
  Michigan beyond 2000.

    "Co-published by arrangement with Hudson Institute"—
T.p. verso.
    Includes bibliographical references.
    1. Economic forecasting—Michigan. 2. Michigan—
Economic policy 3. Michigan—Economic conditions.
I. Title.
HC107.M5H85   1987   338.9774   87-10725
ISBN 0-8191-6462-3 (alk. paper)
ISBN 0-8191-6463-1 (pbk. : alk. paper)

Hudson Institute was founded by the late Herman Kahn in 1961 to examine important issues of public policy. It is a nonprofit, nonpartisan organization; there are no "official" Hudson positions. Its independent and objective analyses address educational, economic, political and national security issues. For additional information: Hudson Institute, Herman Kahn Center, 5395 Emerson Way, P.O. Box 26-919, Indianapolis, IN 46226.

All University Press of America books are produced on acid-free paper which exceeds the minimum standards set by the National Historical Publication and Records Commission.

Acknowledgments

This study was originally undertaken for the Michigan State Senate. Many people were involved in its preparation. Among the Hudson staff who worked on the study, Frank Armbruster, Phil Deluty, Maurice Ernst, Bill Johnston, Carol Kahn, Rob Melnick, Jane Newitt, David Reed, John Tedstrom, and John Thomas made significant contributions. Special thanks is also due to the Hudson support staff; in particular to Yvonne Swinton for her dedication to the preparation of the manuscript.

In Michigan there were hundreds of organizations and individuals who were generous with their time, information and opinions. Special thanks are due to the members of the Advisory Committee who traveled from across the state to review and criticize this work as it progressed. Although their comments and suggestions were invaluable, the Committee members bear no responsibility for the statements, conclusions, or recommendations in this report, which are solely the responsiibility of the Hudson staff members who worked on the project.

Most importantly, special appreciation is due to Majority Leader John Engler, the members of the Michigan State Senate, and their staffs who supported the research team throughout the project. Without their assistance the project could not have been accomplished.

TABLE OF CONTENTS

Preface.	A Futures Study: What and Why	vii
Executive Summary		xiii
I.	Michigan Past and Future	1
II.	The Competition For Industry	17
III.	A Close Look At the Automobile Industry	47
IV.	Demographic Trends	65
V.	Social and Political Trends	81
VI.	Southeast and Outstate Michigan: A Tale of Three Cities	109
VII.	Michigan 2005: Three Perspectives on the Future	129
VIII.	The Policy Choices	145

PREFACE
A FUTURES STUDY: WHAT AND WHY?

All planning and decisionmaking entail assumptions about the future. The experts who advise Michigan on economic development or environmental protection or medical cost containment sometimes make a few of their assumptions explicit, but it is left to the state's elected officials and their staffs to construe the big picture--how it may evolve, what aspects need study and action, and what the aggregate and synergistic effects of a variety of governmental actions are likely to be.

Even when a futures study addresses a specialized question--for example, the long-range outlook for federal aid--it must bring to bear a wide range of evidence. The present study considers many such specific questions, but it also places the pieces into the larger context of Michigan's past, present, and future.

This study differs from many others that have been done in Michigan in that it attempts to synthesize a very broad range of economic, political, social, and cultural trends and to project how they might interact in the state over the next 20 years. It does so by creating a "surprise free scenario"--a description of what the state may be like in the year 2005, given the dynamics of existing and plausible trends, relatively good luck, and good management. It is surprise free only in the sense that "it would not be surprising if things turned out this way," not in the sense that it does not allow for surprises. For, in creating a scenario, it is not sufficient simply to project historic trends. Allowance must be made for response and reaction, and for the intervention of sensible public and private policy actions.

As a supplement to conventional forms of policy research, such a "big picture" study can hope to:

o Spotlight interconnections between policy issues and actions;
o Direct attention to alternative possibilities for the future that can be affected by changes in laws and policies;

- o Help to distinguish problems correctable through normal efforts from those needing special thought and attention;
- o Focus attention on "soft" factors, such as trends in attitudes and values that may have large impacts;
- o Place the present as a moment in historical processes.

These potential assets are accompanied by two obvious liabilities:

- o Because there are no "facts" in the future, but only surmises based on past trends, theories, and analogies, the conclusions of a futures study are bound to reflect the authors' biases;
- o Because the menu of potential surprises is infinitely large, "responsible" futurists always overemphasize the durability of recent trends.

Short of encyclopedic length, this cannot mean touching all the bases every reader considers important. The topics that have been stressed in this study are those that will have the greatest impact on the state's future, and over which the legislature has the most control.

Even the wisest analysts sometimes miss the significance, the magnitude, and even the direction of change. Looking back 20 years (Tables 1 and 2), some of the most plausible and popular forecasts have proved spectacularly wrong. The clouds in the crystal ball are just as heavy for the next 20 years. True surprises could transform this report's "best-guess" scenario. The value of a policy-oriented futures study does not lie in crystal-balling. Its purpose is to provide a resource--a synthesis of data and ideas--that is useful even to those who differ with specific inferences. By viewing the tangle of present concerns from a fresh perspective, and by illustrating new ways of thinking about the future, it can help the reader--the only "futurist" whose forecasts matter--to alter those forecasts intelligently as situations change.

Table 1

In 1964 Would You Have Guessed These Changes?

No. of Housing Units Air-Conditioned	+9,000%
Federal Aid to State/Local Government	+1,400
Price of Gasoline	+ 450
Part-Time College Enrollment	+ 335
Robbery Rate	+ 310
Median Family Income	+ 250
Full-Time College Enrollment	+ 201
Divorce Rate	+ 100
Motor Vehicle Registrations	+ 90
Visits to State Parks	+ 45
No. of Medical Doctors	+ 41
Birth Rate	- 36
Number of Farms	- 42
Infant Mortality Rate	- 46

Table 2

Some Perennial Long-Range Forecasting Errors
(Examples From 20-25 Years Ago)

1. Recent Trends Will Persist

    --The Three-Child Family Will Remain the Norm

    --The Divorce Rate Will Decline

2. Long-Term Trends Will Persist

    --Marriages Will Occur Earlier

    --The Workday and Workweek Will Grow Shorter

3. Rapid Rates of Change Will Slow Down

    --The Entrance of Women Into the Work Force Will Slow

    --Growth in Agricultural Productivity Will Taper Off

    --Improvements in Computer Speed and Price Must Slow Down

4. Laborsaving Machinery Will Reduce Labor Demand

    --Computers in the Office Will Cut the Demand For Secretaries

5. New Technologies Will Not be Rapidly Applied

--Manned Space Travel Will Only be Possible in the 21st Century

6. New Technologies Will be Rapidly Applied

   --Nuclear Energy Will be the Dominant Source of Electric Power by the Turn of the Century

EXECUTIVE SUMMARY

Commitment, hard work, good luck, and good management can make Michigan a competitive, productive, high-tech state by the year 2000. Complacency and inaction are the greatest risks to achieving this goal.

Michigan should be able to:

- o Retain a substantial share of the U.S. automobile industry.
- o Become a major center for new industries, especially robotics and others that utilize the skills and expertise of the automotive industry.
- o Participate in the expansion of those manufacturing and service sectors of the U.S. economy whose location will be determined more by quality of life than by traditional cost considerations.

But these opportunities will be lost unless major progress is made in:

- o Reducing Michigan's high labor costs compared with other states.
- o Creating a generally more favorable business environment.
- o Improving the efficiency of government services.

Such progress will require difficult actions by the Michigan state government. Specifically, it will mean:

- o Shifting expenditures from welfare payments to investments in human and physical capital.
- o Participating actively with labor and management in collective bargaining.
- o Reforming the management and structure of government, if necessary through radical means such a privatization.

o   Developing an effective metropolitan policy for the Detroit area and other Michigan cities.

If Michigan public officials and its residents shed their complacency about the future and their confrontational patterns of the past, they can build a political consensus that can maximize Michigan's comparative advantages.

Michigan in History

For almost two centuries Michigan has been a mirror of the great industrial transition through which the United States has passed. As its economy has evolved from agriculture and fur trading to metals and lumbering, and finally to automobile manufacturing, the state has ridden a roller-coaster from boom to bust to boom.

Time and again during these cycles, pessimistic observers have underestimated the state's capacity to grow and change. During the 1880s, for example, just before the automaking boom was about to begin, one reporter noted that, "many thoughtful Detroiters had made up their minds that the city had probably seen its greatest growth."

But history is on the side of the optimists. With good luck and good management, there is little reason to fear that Michigan's future must be poorer than its past.

The National Trends

Today Michigan stands at the beginning of another great transition. Many of the changes that will occur in the state over the next twenty years are reflections of trends in the national economy. The most important of these include:

o   *The Transition to a Service Economy.* Manufacturing's share of the jobs in Michigan will decline while employment in services rises sharply. Jobs in manufacturing will increasingly involve technical and service skills: research, design,

    engineering, construction, maintenance, marketing and distribution.
- *The End of Geography.* Improvements in transportation and communications, and increases in leisure time are increasingly allowing workplaces and homes to be located anywhere in the world. Michigan must compete with California and Florida for people, and with Japan and Mexico for jobs.
- *The Predominance of Post-Industrial Values.* Like other Americans, people in Michigan are becoming ever more concerned with the quality of their lives. The cleanliness and attractiveness of the environment, the quality of the schools, and the absence of risks such as crime or toxic chemicals are eclipsing economic issues on the public agenda.
- *The Rising Importance of Human Capital.* Physical and financial capital are becoming less important than human knowledge, motivation and organizational skills. Michigan's industries must begin to see their employees more as capital assets, and less as variable costs like energy and steel.
- *The Renewal of the Market Society.* Government programs and policies that have redistributed society's wealth are being cut back. At the same time, a more intensely competitive economy is reducing the broad sharing of risks and incomes that has characterized American society during most of the postwar era. Michigan will need to rely more on its own financial resources as federal aid is retrenced.

Michigan's Competitive Position

How will Michigan fare in the competition for jobs and people? A realistic assessment of the state would list many strengths and some important weaknesses. On the positive side Michigan can count:

- *A Numerous and Rich Population.* Michigan's 9.1 million people comprise the eighth largest market in the country.
- *An Extraordinary Manufacturing Infrastructure.* Michigan is home to a third of the nation's automaking capacity and a substantial fraction of its machine tool and robotics industries.
- *A Skilled Workforce.* Michigan has a high concentration of skilled machinists, tool and die makers, and manufacturing engineers, a large number of chemists, biologists and other scientists, and a growing number of computer hardware and software experts.
- *A Concentration of Powerful Organizations.* Twenty-two Fortune 500 companies are headquartered in the state. The Michigan residents who run these corporations want the state to succeed and have the power and the resources to help accomplish that goal.
- *Abundant Natural Resources.* Michigan has thousands of miles of Great Lakes shoreline, hundreds of smaller lakes, virtually limitless clean water, and one of the largest forest areas in the nation.

Offsetting these substantial assets are several key liabilities:

- *Overdependence on the Automobile Industry.* Thirteen percent of the state's jobs are directly tied to auto production.
- *An Inflated Wage Structure.* High wages in the auto industry have spilled over into most other occupations and industries in the state, making the state less competitive with other regions of the country and the world.

- *A Sense of Complacency.* Decades of boom and bust have conditioned the state's residents to believe that better times are just ahead, making it harder for them to recognize when major changes or sacrifices are needed.
- *A High Level of Factionalism.* The deep divisions between labor and management, Detroit and its suburbs, Republicans and Democrats, and blacks and whites make it hard for the state's citizens to work together to reach shared goals.
- *An Eroding Urban Center.* The long-term decline of the city of Detroit leaves the state in danger of having no central focus for culture, learning, entertainment or retailing.

How do the assets and liabilities add up? While the current resurgence of the state's auto industry has created a mood of optimism, the facts argue that Michigan's competitive position has declined alarmingly in recent years.

In the automobile industry, for example, production is shifting not only overseas, but also to lower cost U.S. plants outside Michigan. Over the last seven years, six foreign automakers have elected to build assembly facilities in the U.S. Only one has chosen Michigan. Coupled with the widely publicized decision by General Motors to locate its Saturn plant in Tennessee, these plants argue that the state has lost its competitive edge as an auto producer. The auto industry is only one aspect of the competition for people and jobs, but its importance to the state's future argues that Michigan must place a high priority on reversing this trend.

Michigan's Future

How will Michigan evolve over the next two decades? The most likely scenario suggests that:

o   *The Michigan economy will continue to grow--pulled along by a strong U.S. economy.* But in contrast to the overall national economy that is projected to grow slightly more than 3 percent annually, Michigan's economy is likely to expand at only about 2.5 percent per year. The state will suffer more severe recessions than the nation as a whole, and per capita income will remain below the national average.

o   *Michigan will continue to be a major manufacturer of automobiles, "smart" industrial tools, and associated products.* Startling advances in the capabilities of robots and other automated manufacturing systems, especially those employing machine vision, advanced sensors, and "artificial intelligence" will enable many Michigan firms to remain on the leading edge of manufacturing technology. Realignment of the yen/dollar relationship, or continued import restraints on Japanese vehicles will prevent the Japanese share of U.S. motor vehicle sales from rising above 35 percent. This retention of manufacturing infrastructure will promote further rapid growth of service industries, ranging from accounting and computer programming to retailing and restaurants.

o   *Despite the continued importance of manufacturing to the state's economy, factory employment will not increase.* Even if auto sales grow steadily, and markets for other Michigan products such as office furniture or robots expand rapidly, employment in manufacturing will remain stable at just over one million. In Michigan, as in the rest of the country, highly automated manufacturing plants will produce more with fewer workers. In the auto industry, for example, half as many workers will be needed to produce the same number of vehicles. Employment in services will climb rapidly, however, more than making up for the stagnant level of factory jobs. By 2005, more than three-fourths of the jobs in Michigan will be service jobs and more people will be working in the finance, real estate and insurance businesses than in auto manufacturing.

o *As the number of manufacturing jobs shrink, the skills required of the remaining workers will rise.* The average production worker in the year 2005 will need to understand mathematics and statistics, the use of computers, and basic engineering concepts.

o *Fewer people will live in the state.* Out-migration, particularly of the young and able, will shrink the state's population slightly, both absolutely and relative to the rest of the country. On average, people living in Michigan are likely to be older, with the largest increases coming among those age 45-60. In the redistricting following the year 2000 census, Michigan will emerge with only 15 representatives in Congress.

o *Michigan's residents will be much more dispersed.* Many parts of the state, particularly in the southwest, may experience a boom, while Detroit and some of its near-in suburbs languish. If current trends continue, by the year 2005 there will be more people living in the Grand Rapids SMSA (Kent and Ottawa counties) than remain in the city of Detroit.

o *Black people, particularly those living in Detroit, will face the greatest difficulties as a result of the changes in Michigan's economy.* Every major change that Michigan can expect--the relative decline of factory wages and the loss of factory jobs, the cutbacks in federal support, the need for better-educated workers, and the continuing erosion of Detroit--will hurt blacks more than whites. Detroit--which will be almost four-fifths

black by 2005--will face a continuous cycle of fiscal crises.
o *A much smaller share of state and local budgets in Michigan will be funded by federal programs.* The state will be forced to rely more on its own tax base, and to take more responsibility for regulating business.
o *Detroit's cycle of deterioration is likely to have begun to turn around by 2005.* Building outward from a core of development along the riverfront, and relying during the early stages mostly on its own resources, the black community of Detroit will have gradually begun to turn the city and its institutions around. Black leaders who are independent of legislators in Lansing and Washington, not patient with racism as an explanation for problems, and willing to challenge the old political rules, as well as their own constituency, will initiate a revitalization. Though early progress will be slow, the direction will be unmistakable by the year 2005. Meanwhile, the trends in near-in suburbs--aging populations, rapid racial changes, and declining tax bases--will have become the new focus of concern.

These projections of a more exurban, white collar, better educated, high-tech Michigan depend on a number of plausible but relatively optimistic assumptions. Alternatively, if import restraints on Japanese cars are eliminated, or if Japanese auto plants in the U.S. increase their sales more rapidly than expected, General Motors, Ford and Chrysler plants in the state could close, leading to sustained recession-level unemployment and rapid out-migration from the state. If Michigan loses the lead in manufacturing automation to other states or nations, its most important bridge to the future will be severed.

Many of the uncertainties in Michigan's future are downside risks. Achieving the outcomes in this scenario will require both good luck and good management.

The Policy Choices

Over many years, the great wealth created by the automobile industry in Michigan has focused attention on issues of equity: the distribution of the tax burden, the division of revenues between wages and profits, the rights of poor and disadvantaged people. These issues are still important today. But the next two decades will require far more attention to questions of efficiency and competitiveness in addition to those of fairness. Old habits of thinking and traditional relationships must change, particularly those built around adversarial thinking and protection of long-standing rights.

Complacency and inaction are the greatest risks. Three years ago in the depths of a frightening recession, there was a widely shared sense of the need for change. Today the return to normalcy is almost complete: both political parties are hurrying to cut taxes, Chrysler workers are back to wage parity with workers at General Motors and Ford, and most of the laid-off auto workers have returned to work. If Michigan fails to come to terms with the need for major changes in policies and attitudes, the state can expect painful, unplanned changes to be forced on it.

What changes are needed? How can Michigan increase its chances of prospering economically and socially over the next two decades? The greatest opportunities lie in four areas:
- o Regaining the Advantage as a Manufacturer of Automobiles
- o Delivering Government Services More
- o Attracting People to Michigan
- o Adopting Metropolitan Policies for Michigan's Cities

REGAINING THE ADVANTAGE AS A MANUFACTURER OF AUTOMOBILES

Michigan cannot protect its lead in automobile production, it must regain it. How can this be done?

o   *Readjust the Wage Structure to Reflect Competitive Realities.* The higher wages paid to workers in the automobile industry, and to others in Southeast Michigan, are at the heart of the problem of competitiveness. Over the next twenty years these high wages will either be brought into line as a result of union negotiations, or automotive production will gradually shift to lower wage firms in other parts of the country and the world. Michigan must ensure that wage adjustments occur at home before automotive production moves away.

Although most of the decisions that can affect Michigan's wage structure are in the hands of union and management leaders, the state government can be a more active participant in the bargaining process. For example, the state might offer to shoulder more of the costs of training that are now paid by companies. It can also do more to hold down health care costs, and the costs of its own workforce.

o   *Continue the Effort to Reduce Business Costs.* Over the past several years state policy makers have vigorously debated issues such as workers' compensation, unemployment insurance, and business taxes. Until the state has reduced these costs below the levels prevailing in competing states, there will be more to be done.

o   *Become a Full Partner with Labor and Management in the Drive for Competitiveness.* In its quest for the Saturn plant, Michigan proposed a far-reaching partnership with General Motors and the UAW. This program involved a fresh approach to state regulatory policies, investment in site development and worker training, and programs to develop the support base of suppliers. This was a sensible and dynamic strategy. Despite the fact that the effort failed to attract the Saturn complex, this program, particularly its regulatory, training, and research components, should be implemented now on an industry-wide basis.

o   *Increase State Investments in Advanced Technologies and Engineering Education.* Michigan has already made a substantial commitment to developing its high technology research capabilities, particularly in the areas of robotics, computer integrated manufacturing and new materials. The scale of the state's investment still does not match the importance of these technologies. Michigan should be prepared to spend much more heavily to attract the leading educators and the most talented students in these areas. The state should not accept the possibility of being second in these technologies.

DELIVERING GOVERNMENT SERVICES MORE EFFICIENTLY

Over the next twenty years Michigan will be under constant pressure to deliver its services more efficiently. Two basic strategies deserve consideration:

o   *Privatize Some Public Services.* An increasing number of state and local governments are beginning to experiment with contracting arrangements for the delivery of government services. Although there are risks and political difficulties associated with these steps, the benefits of contracting outweigh the costs. By bringing the discipline of the marketplace to bear on public services, the system provides automatic correction for the rigidities in wages, work rules, and benefit structures that creep into government institutions. Not only can contractors often perform given jobs better and more cheaply, the challenge of competition often leads to rapid improvements in the efficiency and cost-effectiveness of the public bureaucracy. Even an experimental program can have far-reaching impacts on the cost and quality of government services.

The obvious candidates for privatization include the operation of the correctional system, the administration of state funded health programs, and the management of state welfare and unemployment insurance programs. At the local level not only traditional candidates such as trash collection, but unconventional ones such as fire, police, and even public education, might potentially be contracted.

o   *Adopt an Investment Strategy to Reallocate State Spending.* State government spending may be roughly divided into two categories: programs that support current consumption, such as income support and public services; and programs with long term returns, such as highways, economic development and education. Over the past 15 years Michigan's spending has been increasingly biased toward consumption rather than investment. For example, Michigan spent 29 percent more per capita on welfare than the average for all other states in 1983, and its welfare spending has grown almost twice as fast as the national average since 1970. By contrast, Michigan's education spending, which was 32 percent above the national average in 1970 was only 10 percent above the norm in 1983.

These priorities should be reversed. Specifically, Michigan's capital programs in the areas of education, transportation, advanced training, and industry development deserve higher priority, and those aimed at providing social and public services, and income transfers deserve more careful scrutiny.

ATTRACTING PEOPLE TO MICHIGAN

Over the next two decades many more people will be free to choose where they want to live. Michigan has many advantages in the competition for these people, particularly in comparison with some of its midwestern neighbors.

In order to better exploit its natural advantages, Michigan should seek to attract and hold those people who have the greatest choice of where to live: college students, young professionals, and retirees. In addition, the state should focus more attention on developing the facilities needed to attract tourists to the state.

Because Michigan's population will be aging over the next twenty years, and because the auto industry is likely to use retirement as one of the main mechanisms for shrinking its workforce, the state has particularly great interest in enhancing its status as a retirement center. Whether the large numbers of social security and pension checks due to auto industry retirees are mailed to addresses in Tucson or Traverse City will have great impact on the economic health of the state over the next twenty years. To promote substantial new tourist and retirement development the state might consider reallocating or increasing its spending for parks and recreation and for highway and air transportation facilities serving leisure areas. Tax policies that discourage retirement in the state (e.g., inheritance taxes) might also be revised.

Similarly, the state can do more to encourage young people to choose Michigan as a place to live. For example, college tuition for both in- and out-of-state residents should be based on the strategic objective of attracting students, not just on budgetary necessities. As the California system has demonstrated, inexpensive, high-quality education can be a tool for encouraging people to move to the state, as well as a boon to industry.

Chapter I
MICHIGAN PAST AND FUTURE

A. History's Mirror

For almost two centuries Michigan has been a mirror of the great industrial transition through which the United States has passed.

At the beginning of the 19th century Michigan, like much of the rest of America, was populated by a few, relatively poor people who lived largely at the mercy of nature. When the famous French chronicler of life in America, Alexis de Tocqueville, traveled into the deep wilderness north of Saginaw in 1830, he found a tiny band of pioneers struggling to stay alive in a forest clearing at the edge of the known world.

Like the rest of the nation, Michigan grew during the 1800s mostly by exploiting its rich heritage of natural resources. Abundant wildlife and farmable land drew fur trappers, traders and homesteaders. With the development of the railroad, the demand for Michigan's iron, copper and lumber exploded, creating a series of economic booms. Each new surge of industrial development brought a new wave of immigrants to the state from the east, and created vast new wealth among the state's residents.

So rapidly were these assets depleted, however, that Michigan could not sustain its prosperity by relying solely on natural resources. With alarming regularity each boom was followed by bust when resources gave out or demand slackened. In 1808, at the height of the fur boom, John Jacob Astor founded the American Fur Company; by 1834 the company had been dissolved.

Even before this last boom was winding down and the final logs from Michigan's once great forests were floating downriver to become houses in the suburbs of Chicago and Cleveland, the seeds of a new industrial order were springing up. In southeastern Michigan, an enormous variety of manufacturing enterprises had emerged serving regional and national markets. Shipbuilders, drug and chemical manufacturers, wagon and piano makers, the world's largest stove making factory, and a host of other businesses were thriving in Detroit and other Michigan cities.

Among the machinists who manned these factories the dying lumber industry was less important than a new technology with which many were tinkering--the internal combustion engine. In a few years these tinkerers, backed by Michigan capitalists investing fortunes accumulated in earlier years, kicked off the greatest boom of all. Soon the automobile business transformed the state from a series of decaying mill towns amid the cutover forests to a manufacturing complex so extraordinary that it became the image of modern industrialism.

The automobile industry that flowered in Michigan not only set the world's standard for manufacturing efficiency and changed the nation's way of life, it also established a new standard for worker wages and benefits, for social justice and for the rights of workers to organize and bargain collectively. The singular success of American capitalism in creating a blue collar middle class, rather than a rebellious proletariat as Marx had predicted, was a story that unfolded in Michigan.

Today, Michigan's nine million residents are generally rich by world standards and largely in control of the forces of nature. The automobiles, airplanes, telephones, televisions, refrigerators and air conditioners that are commonplace in their lives have freed them from the limits that geography, weather, hunger, and sickness once imposed. Today, many families on welfare in Detroit have powers and choices that Louis XIV could not command.

This historic sketch is important not just because it illustrates the degree to which Michigan has been a paradigm of the great transition from general poverty to widespread wealth in the United States. It also argues powerfully against fears that Michigan's future must be poorer than its past. Time and again the wisest observers have underestimated the state's capacity to change and grow. Though there are certainly unsettling and even threatening changes ahead, history is on the

MICHIGAN PAST AND FUTURE

side of the optimists. During the nationwide depression of the 1880s, for example, when Detroit had lost its importance as a shipping port and appeared to be sliding downhill compared to other cities in the Midwest, "many thoughtful Detroiters had made up their minds that the city had probably seen its greatest growth. At best, it was a lopsided city, flanking Canada, and off the main lines of the transcontinental railroad."[1] One thoughtful Detroiter of the time, Henry Utley, who headed the public library, completely missed the entrepreneurial dynamism that was about to transform southeastern Michigan, when he described his home town as "rather slow and unenterprising."[2]

Even some of the initial backers of the auto business underestimated its potential by staggering margins. As Eugene F. Cooley, an early investor in the Michigan auto industry, later recalled: "I am sure I did not see any great future for the invention, and I do not think others did, but we felt that, if developed, the power vehicles would have some sale, and that a business possibly could be developed which would show a profit."[3]

When 21st century historians review the 1980s, they are likely to find as many similar doubts or miscalculations of the potentials of new technologies and industries. "Barring bad luck and bad management," as the late futurist Herman Kahn was fond of saying, the future of Michigan is likely to be better than its past.

B. Michigan Today

If history provides a vantage point from which to view Michigan's future, the present supplies some of the details that

---

[1]Merrill Denison, *The Power to Go* (Garden City, N.Y.: Doubleday, 1956).
[2]George S. May, *A Most Unique Machine: The Michigan Origins of the American Automobile Industry* (WIlliam B. Erdmans Publishing Company, 1975), p. 76.
3. *Ibid*, p. 63.

in the Detroit machine shops and Flint lumber fortunes of the 1880s, the future of Michigan in 1985 is partly visible in the skills of its people, and in the financial and organizational capacities of the state's giant corporations, unions and other institutions. Much of what Michigan will be in the 21st century is already in place.

If Michigan were a business, its current balance sheet would list a substantial number of assets. Compared to the rest of the United States and the Midwest, "Michigan, Inc." can count:

- o   A numerous and rich population. In 1983 the 9.1 million residents of Michigan received $105 billion of personal income making the state the eight largest market in the country.
- o   An extraordinary manufacturing infrastructure. With more than 1,000,000 manufacturing jobs, a third of the nation's auto making capability, and a substantial fraction of the robotics and machine tool industries, Michigan has heavy manufacturing assets that are unequalled in the U.S.
- o   A concentration of powerful organizations. Michigan is home to 22 of the Fortune 500 largest industrial corporations in America, as well as to the United Auto Workers, and the largest Blue Cross/Blue Shield organization in the country. A small number of Michigan residents have the power to make far-reaching decisions about the state's future.
- o   A skilled workforce. Michigan not only has a high concentration of skilled machinists, tool and die makers, and manufacturing engineers; it has a large number of chemists, biologists, and other scientists, and a growing number of computer hardware and software experts.
- o   Abundant natural resources. Michigan has thousands of miles of Great Lakes shoreline,

hundreds of smaller lakes, virtually limitless clean water, one of the largest forest areas east of the Mississippi, and substantial deposits of iron and other minerals.

Offsetting these substantial assets are several liabilities:

o Overdependence on a single manufacturing industry. Despite repeated calls for diversification, 13 percent of the state's jobs are directly tied to automobile production, and a much higher fraction are indirectly related to this key business.
o An inflated wage structure. The success of the automobile industry in Michigan has escalated the wages of all workers in the state compared to those elsewhere in the region and the nation. The ability of existing industries to compete, and the state's ability to attract, hold and grow new businesses is harmed by this ubiquitous wage and benefit inflation.
o A sense of complacency. Accustomed to decades of bust followed by boom, the state's residents and its leaders often assume that "things will get back to normal when the economy picks up." While this is generally true, it is a belief that makes it hard to recognize when changes are needed.
o A high level of factionalism. The divisions between labor and management, Detroit and its suburbs, Republicans and Democrats, and blacks and whites are deeper and more harmful in Michigan than in many other states. Without a unifying vision or collective agreement on what problems need attention, cooperative action is hard to achieve in the state.
o An eroding urban center. The long term decline of Detroit leaves the state in danger of having no

central geographic focus for culture, learning, entertainment, employment and retailing. While it is certainly possible to continue to distribute these activities across the state, many of the scale economies and self-reinforcing growth that comes from concentration of such resources will be lost if this pattern continues.

C. Michigan's Future

How will these assets and liabilities change over the next two decades? What will life be like in Michigan in the year 2005? To answer these questions it is important to define the external forces that will affect the state. Michigan in the 21st century will have been powerfully shaped by five great trends operating in the United States today:

o   The Transition to a Service Economy.

o   The End of Geography.

o   The Predominance of Post-Industrial Values.

o   The Rising Importance of Human Capital.

o   The Revival of the Market Society.

1. The Transition to a Service Economy

In 1980 the share of the nation's workforce officially classified as "white-collar" climbed above 50 percent, while traditional blue collar jobs fell below one third. The majority of workers no longer report to the factory, but to the office. Only 30 percent of the nation's jobs are connected with goods producing industries, while 70 percent provide services.

While this shift to service jobs has been underway for more than half a century, the transformation of the economy is not yet complete. Over the next two decades these trends will continue and perhaps accelerate, in a pattern that will resemble the decline of agricultural employment earlier in the century. Just as agricultural jobs dropped from 21 percent to 12 percent of the labor force between 1930 and 1950, so the share of manufacturing employment may drop from today's level of 21 percent to 12-14 percent in 2005.

As a society we will be increasingly involved in activities that have less to do with goods production than with information transfer and manipulation, leisure and entertainment, education, health care and other services. The wealth management and redistribution sectors--law, accounting, real estate, finance and insurance--will grow rapidly. Among those who are still involved in the manufacturing sector, activities will continue to shift away from the production process both upstream to research, design, engineering and tooling, and downstream to distribution, marketing and sales.

Michigan has, of course, already been affected by these changes. But the changes expected in the next twenty years are likely to be more substantial for the state than for much of the rest of the country. By 2005 only about 22 percent of all jobs in Michigan will be in manufacturing compared to 29 percent today, with direct automotive manufacturing jobs dropping from 320,000 to 200,000. Health care, travel and tourism, retail trade, communications and other services are likely to become the dominant sources of employment in the state.

These trends have major implications for Michigan. Declining auto employment will weaken the position of the United Auto Workers both by reducing their numbers, and possibly by forcing a continuation of wage and work rule concessions, as the industry struggles to regain its competitive position. Unions in general may become less influential as employment shifts to less organized occupations. Wage premiums (compared to other states) will also decline as a result of the shift away from high wage manufacturing to lower wage service jobs, the slower rate of growth of manufacturing wages, and slack labor markets.

MICHIGAN BEYOND 2000

2. The End of Geography

Advances in transportation and communications, and the increase in leisure time have combined to release society almost completely from the restrictions that geography once imposed on the location of workplaces, homes, and stores. A few decades ago, factories were sited near sources of raw materials or markets, homes were near jobs, and retailing followed residential development with a certainty that was treated as a science.

Today, it is often possible for new factories to be located anywhere in the world. Corporate headquarters and research facilities can be moved on the whim of the chief executive. Homes can be located tens or hundreds of miles away from workplaces connected by superhighways, communications or air travel. Huge retailing facilities can prosper in the woods of Maine (L.L. Bean) or the plains of South Dakota (Walls Drug). There are promotions that encourage New Yorkers to fly to London to take advantage of Harrods post-Christmas sales.

Increases in leisure time have added a new dimension to this geographic freedom. Retirement communities grow and prosper in Florida, Arizona, and Hawaii without an industrial underpinning. Attractive resorts can be created from wilderness areas to serve convention and vacation industries. These sites can support huge numbers of visitors for varying periods of time, feed them delicacies grown thousands of miles away, house them in controlled environments, entertain or inform them and return them home--supported entirely by income generated elsewhere in the country or the world.

The rapid evolution of communications technology will soon add another dimension to this geographic freedom. By the late 1990s a high capacity, digital telephone network will be almost fully deployed across the country, enabling instant, low cost transfers of huge quantities of information. The potential to deliver reports, newspapers, magazines, music, pictures, video conferences, or other material electronically will further expand the horizons of businesses and residences to relocate.

For Michigan these trends pose a profound challenge. Most importantly, the shrinking world means that the U.S. auto

MICHIGAN PAST AND FUTURE

market is no longer protected by geography from international competitors. While today's challenge comes from Japan, tomorrow's may arise in Korea, China or some other nation.

The mirror image of this competition is that American auto producers are less and less tied to production facilities in Michigan. While auto production is somewhat more immobile than many lighter industries, it too is increasingly independent of geographic restraints. Though the reduced inventory production systems currently in vogue call for highly integrated production facilities, these large units of production are no longer bound to the state by history or geographic necessity. Recently, Volkswagen, Nissan, Toyota, Mitsubishi and Honda, have all built or are building large assembly facilities outside the state.

In addition, the shift to a service economy means that the location of many types of job producing activities that will be important to Michigan, such as corporate management, research and development, tourism and retailing will depend on how attractive the state is as a place to live, work and visit. As the limits of geography recede further, the state will be in declared as well as unspoken competition with many other places in the world to attract people and jobs.

In order to succeed, the state must become cost competitive with other states and regions in terms of wages and business costs. It must also build on activities or attributes in which it has an advantage. For example, it is unlikely that Detroit can compete against Chicago as a regional financial center, but it is very plausible that Michigan's lake frontage can become a regional magnet for tourism and conventions. Diversification by General Motors, Ford or Chrysler is much more likely to bring new industries to the state than tax funded economic development incentives.

Locational independence also means that Detroit's future will be determined less by its history and size than by how well the city manages to reestablish itself as a center of culture, education or entertainment. Unless current trends are reversed or the state government intervenes it is possible that Detroit will become a suburb of one of its current neighbors in the next twenty years.

3. The Predominance of Post-Industrial Values

The affluence and leisure that many Americans enjoy is likely to spread over the next two decades, bringing a measure of wealth to a growing majority of citizens. During the 21st century most Americans are likely to enjoy a higher standard of living than they do today. They will certainly spend longer in school, both before and during their work lives. They are likely to have greater choices to retire early. Their work week is likely to be shorter, either because of increases in holidays or because of a shift to service occupations that have shorter hours.

This growth of leisure and relative wealth will change the values and attitudes of society, promoting far reaching changes in politics, lifestyles, and laws. Michigan will be deeply affected by the trends.

What are these emerging post-industrial values?

Looked at from one perspective, post-industrial values are simply widespread extensions of traditional American beliefs and expectations. In addition to life, liberty, the pursuit of happiness and the Bill of Rights, post-industrial Americans generally believe in the right to sophisticated medical care, to a publicly supported education, to inexpensive and safe consumer products, to hold a decent paying job, and to a comfortable retirement at age 65.

Rights may seem to be an extravagant word for these expectations, and no doubt they would fail if presented as planks at a constitutional convention. But a great majority of Americans behave as though they were ratified. With these basics taken for granted, growing numbers of Americans in the late 20th century feel that the quality of life--measured in terms of educational and recreational opportunity, climate, the beauty of the surroundings, friendships, challenging jobs, and other subjective factors--should be the key determinants of

MICHIGAN PAST AND FUTURE

where and how they live. For many people, economic choices no longer dictate behavior as they once did.

Looked at in another light, the central assumption in post-industrial America is the belief that life should generally be free of risk and inconvenience: good diet or exercise or medical care can postpone the infirmities of age; government regulations can eliminate the dangers of driving cars or the uncertainties of buying consumer products; every risk--from cancer to law suits--can be insured against.

The assumption that money and advanced technology should be able to solve all problems in a post-industrial society makes the persistence of problems such as crime and freeway congestion particularly nettlesome. "If we can go to the moon, why can't we..." is the often heard refrain.

At their worst, these risk averse attitudes can be powerful inhibitors of change and development. The NIMBY (Not-In-My-Backyard) environmentalists who indiscriminately resist all investments in new roads or industrial plants may indefinitely postpone construction of facilities that would benefit society as a whole. And government regulation driven by public aversion to risks can add so much sand to the gears of industry that they may permanently slow down.

What will these values and expectations mean to Michigan? First, they mean that state government will become increasingly involved in the debates and trade-offs that are generated by lifestyle considerations. So far, many of the regulations and programs that grew out of environmentalism, health concerns, consumerism and other expressions of post-industrial values saw their first expression at the federal level. But many of the issues are inherently state or local matters. Michigan, which has not had to face some of the most complex issues of costs and benefits because of federal preemption, will find that the state must increasingly take the lead.

The strictly economic issues--are property taxes too high, should unemployment benefits be reduced--are likely to be superseded in the political debate by the new concern over the environment, toxic chemicals, the uneven quality of the schools, or the persistence of crime. Although economic issues will

11

always rise to the surface during recessions, the most sustained debates will center around lifestyle issues.

Secondly, the growing predominance of these values means that Michigan's economic success will increasingly depend on how well it responds to them. When huge majorities of Americans feel that they shouldn't have to put up with polluted lakes, poor schools, toxic chemicals or crime, they will vote with their feet on these issues. States or jurisdictions that cannot offer the amenities and environments that many demand will lose population relative to those that can. These trends will become particularly marked if interest rates fall significantly, since traditional American mobility has been inhibited in recent years by the high costs of new home financing.

One aspect of lifestyle concerns is of particular importance to Michigan: the leisure opportunities that the state offers. With less and less of each person's life spent chained to the desk or assembly line, more and more time and money are spent on non-work pursuits. Michigan has a great stake in whether it remains the place to go for three day weekends, summer vacations, higher education and retirement. A massive early retirement program in the automobile industry, for example, could be almost as damaging to the state's economy as widespread layoffs, if the retirees choose to move to Florida to receive their checks. Similarly, an unemployment program that allows workers to leave the state while still collecting benefits, or enables them to receive lump sum payments to relocate could have the same negative effects.

4. The Rising Importance of Human Capital

A thousand years ago the wealth of kingdoms was measured in gold, gems and other fine objects in the treasury. More recently, the wealth of nations has been judged mostly on the basis of industrial capital--factories, processing plants, and other installations capable of producing goods.

As the striking rebirth of the economies of Europe and Japan after World War II illustrated, however, the capacity to produce wealth depends as much on knowledge, skills, and organizations as on tools, factories and other capital. Today, there is growing recognition of the overwhelming importance of human capital, compared to the declining role of physical plants, as the sources of wealth.

Though machines are certainly important, and can substitute for people in some jobs, the fundamental evolution of the economy is in exactly the opposite direction: the more the production of goods is automated the more the creation of wealth depends on human labor, both physical and mental. The value in a can of Coke is barely related to the cost of the ingredients, but rather is created primarily by the people who manage the enormous advertising and distribution network maintained by the company. Similarly, the fastest growing American industry, health care, though it relies on many sophisticated labor and life saving technologies, basically depends on human skills. In the computer industry, where automation has been carried to the highest degree, human capital is at the heart of every company and product. As a top executive of a large Silicon Valley manufacturer put it: "Our corporate assets leave the building each night at 5:30."

The growing dominance of knowledge as the source of wealth is not fully understood by some in government and industry. States that continue to focus primarily on landing manufacturing plants, rather than on attracting human capital (from artists to engineers) are positioning themselves on the trailing edge of economic change. Companies that continue to behave as though their competitive advantage depends primarily on their superior facilities or capital resources rather than on the abilities and motivation of their research, marketing or production people are likely to become losers in the marketplace.

For Michigan, the shift to human capital has major implications. The Michigan automobile industry, in particular, faces an enormous task in converting its historic view of itself as a capital intensive industry in which most employees are variable cost inputs (like energy or steel) to a model in which all employees are viewed as assets. And because auto industry labor relations are such a pervasive backdrop for other Michigan industries, new or existing companies within the state face the same challenge of evolving away from the legacy of combative labor relations toward new models of organization and human resource management.

The organizations that deliver state and local services within the state face the same challenge. For example, the advancement of educational quality within the state is likely to depend less on the dollars devoted to classrooms and computers than on the ability of school boards to attract and motivate high quality teachers and professors. Similarly, the quality of the "business environment" within the state may depend less on specific tax incentives than on the consistency and competency with which state bureaucracies serve or regulate business.

5. The Renewal of the Market Society

Through most of the twentieth century, social progress has been measured in part by the development of mechanisms to redistribute wealth, share opportunities and provide collectively for society's members. Government, of course, has been the primary instrument of this process through the tax system and programs such as social security, medicare, unemployment insurance and welfare, as well as through a variety of economic regulatory regimes. Many other institutions have also played a part. Insurance plans, for example, transfer income from the healthy to the sick and from the fortunate to the unfortunate. Unions have often ensured that all of their members were paid according to the classification of the job, rather than according to the skills or experience of the employee, leading to a more equal sharing of employee incomes within companies or industries. Electric and telephone utilities often transfer income from business to residential users, and from urban to rural residents.

Taken together, these mechanisms have become a fundamental part of our social fabric, and have led to a much more equal sharing of society's wealth than would exist in a pure market economy.

MICHIGAN PAST AND FUTURE

Beginning in the 1970s, a number of parallel trends emerged which began to significantly alter some of these mechanisms. Foremost was the trend toward economic deregulation by government. Transportation and telecommunications deregulation, for example, had the effect of ending many cross--subsidies once sanctioned by government. Reductions in the rate of growth of social programs, and in federal aid to states and cities, reduced the government transfers of income between regions and between segments of society. Shifts in the structure of the economy weakened union control over wages, leading to less uniformity in the distribution of labor income.

Over the next decade or longer, these trends are likely to continue and perhaps accelerate. A national reassessment of the role of the federal government has undermined the consensus for further wealth sharing mechanisms. The narrowing gap between regional incomes has reduced the need and justification for programs to promote regional equality. A return to the notion of individual responsibility--whether to provide for retirement or to drive safely--has lessened the thrust toward broad sharing of risks and income. Continued deregulation driven both by technology and changing attitudes--can be expected in finance, transportation, utility regulation, broadcasting, telecommunications and other government controlled industries. The role of unions is likely to shrink further, as structural changes combine with more participative management styles to reduce union memberships; and improving information and transportation technology is likely to lead to more competitive markets, as consumers are offered a wider array of competitive alternatives.

For Michigan, the revival of the market society presents new responsibilities and choices for the state government. Most importantly, the state will need to become more self-reliant on its own financial resources as federal aid is retrenched. And to the extent that federal deregulation runs ahead of the Michigan electorate, the state will have to grapple with issues of fairness ranging from "lifeline" telephone rates for poor rural residents to increased state assistance for Detroit.

Chapter 2

THE COMPETITION FOR INDUSTRY

A. Michigan's Economy in Transition--An Overview

The economy of the State of Michigan is so highly concentrated in the manufacture of automobiles and activities that support the automobile industry that the future of the state and the industry are inextricably linked. Those basic industries, including non-electrical machinery, primary metals, and others, are going through a fundamental transition. The success with which those industries make that transition will determine the fate of the state's economy over the next twenty years. No amount of diversification or growth in other industries can alter this situation.

A successful transition to a post-industrial economy in Michigan does not mean a diminution of manufacturing activity or the wealth that such activity generates in the state. Quite the contrary, it means a return to competitiveness of the state's industries based on new state-of-the-art processes and production technology, and new products incorporating advanced materials and design concepts. Even though manufacturing output will increase, traditional blue collar employment will decline. To the extent that employment is maintained in manufacturing, its nature will change in important ways. Many fewer workers will be employed in routine machining, stamping, forging, assembly, materials handling and inspection activities. More may be involved in equipment maintenance, production control, quality control, and other non-routine functions. Manufacturing employment in product design and development, product testing, marketing, finance and other non-production activities may be less affected by the incorporation of advanced automation, and is likely to become a higher proportion of total manufacturing employment.

MICHIGAN BEYOND 2000

1. The Dow Chemical Case

Historians looking back from the perspective of 2005 will likely notice striking similarities between the evolution of the Michigan auto industry and the pattern at an earlier industrial complex: the Dow Chemical Company's facilities in Midland. Between the early 1960s and 1985 Dow's hourly workforce in Michigan was halved, while the share of workers with scientific and engineering backgrounds grew rapidly. Even the least educated Dow workers are now required to have passed high school chemistry and physics, and to understand basic mathematics. Despite a divisive strike and repeated layoffs, most workers in Dow's Midland plants recognize that they are involved in global competition, and that their personal success is inextricably interlocked with the success of the company. The product mix has also undergone significant change, shifting from bulk chemicals and brine-based products, to specialty, consumer and petrochemical products. Despite these fundamental changes in workers, products and processes, the main Dow facilities have stayed in Michigan--partly because longtime Michigan residents were determined to see their communities prosper.

If the world auto industry in the year 2005 remains centered in Michigan, it is likely to have undergone a similar process: an upgrading of the skills of workers; major accommodations by unions and management leading to a shared vision of corporate and individual success, a shift in the type of work from brawn to brain, and a parallel upscaling of the product. In the end, decisions by auto industry and union leaders--most of whom live in Michigan--will determine whether these tumultuous changes take place in Michigan or outside of it.

The implications of a successful transition to a post-industrial economy in Michigan may be unpalatable for many, particularly for workers who face radical changes in their pay, or in the nature of the work they do. The implications of a failed transition are even less palatable. If Michigan's basic industries do not find more efficient and competitive ways to produce better products the state and its workforce could suffer catastrophic losses of plants, jobs and people.

THE COMPETITION FOR INDUSTRY

2. Non-Auto Related Industries

Other economic sectors besides the auto and related industries will play important roles as well. The non-manufacturing sectors, that is, services and government, will undoubtedly experience the greatest growth rates in Michigan, though at best only at rates comparable to their growth nationally. The growth of non-manufacturing employment is characteristic of the transition to a post-industrial economy, and has been evident in Michigan for at least twenty years. The trend will continue, especially in medical services, communications and information services, food services, and government. Other segments of the non-manufacturing sector that are likely to experience healthy growth in output, but not necessarily in employment, are financial services (especially consumer services), personal services, and utility services.

These trends mirror national ones, but the development of a service-based economy in Michigan may take on a unique, auto-influenced twist. Just as the auto industry can serve as a nexus for the development of new generations of automated production equipment, it may also spur the creation of an entirely new approach to manufacturing management, communication, and control. Current computer and communications hardware is already capable of eliminating most paper flow in the manufacturing process. The provision of the software and other services that would permit manufacturers to take full advantage of this possibility could itself become an important industry. The auto companies will probably lead the way in the implementation of paperless manufacturing (e.g., GM-EDS) and every effort should be made to ensure that this crucial development is exploited as thoroughly as possible in Michigan.

B. Michigan's Economy in Midwestern and U.S. Contexts

The evolution of Michigan's economy is, of course, taking place in the context of economic upheaval and change throughout the nation and the world. The early stages of the industrial revolution saw the creation of the technologies that made it possible to produce ever-increasing quantities of agricultural and manufactured products with more efficiency and less physical effort. The latter stages are extending this process, shifting labor to service industries and increasing individual leisure.

While most developed countries are entering a post-industrial era, a variety of countries are advancing rapidly toward full industrialization. These countries are proving to be formidable competition in world markets, particularly in certain basic industries.

These effects are clearly illustrated in U.S. employment data. In the 1970s and into the 1980s, employment in manufacturing has declined by approximately 1 million workers (see Table 2-1). While the recent recession certainly affected this result, it is apparent that the long-term trend of employment growth in manufacturing has at least flattened. In contrast to the employment figures, industrial output increased by more than one half during the same period.

The employment growth in the U.S. that did occur during this period was in non-manufacturing sectors, particularly in services and retail sales. Nineteen million new jobs were created in this sector between 1970 and 1983, representing an increase of 30 percent. This growth permitted the U.S. to record overall employment growth of 23 percent, despite the loss of manufacturing jobs.

The economy of the East North Central region (Indiana, Illinios, Michigan, Ohio and Wisconsin) is more heavily concentrated in manufacturing than the nation as a whole (see Table 2-2). The region accounted for more than one quarter of the nation's manufacturing employment in 1970, but less than one-fifth of its total employment and population. The major manufacturing industries in the region are basic industries such as primary metals and autos, which have been subjected to the fiercest foreign competition. Nonetheless, the decline in manufacturing employment in the region was unexpectedly disproportionate. The East North Central region actually lost more manufacturing jobs between 1970 and 1983 than the total of all manufacturing jobs lost in the rest of the country. The

THE COMPETITION FOR INDUSTRY

Table 2-1

EMPLOYMENT DISTRIBUTION BY SECTOR, U.S., EAST NORTH CENTRAL REGION, MICHIGAN, SELECTED YEARS 1970-1983

	1970 No.	%	1975 No.	%	1980 No.	%	1983 No.	%
Total Employment	77,244	100.0	82,545	100.0	95,142	100.0	95,235	100.0
Manufacturing	19,410	25.1	18,320	22.2	20,354	21.4	18,435	19.4
Durables	11,254	14.6	10,694	13.0	12,226	12.9	10,727	11.3
Autos	813	1.1	786	1.0	798	0.8	748	0.8
Primary Metals	1,314	1.7	1,143	1.4	1,151	1.2	829	0.9
Non-Elect. Machinery	1,982	2.6	2,062	2.5	2,486	2.6	2,031	2.1
Fabricated Metals	1,384	1.8	1,460	1.8	1,614	1.7	1,368	1.4
Non-Durables	8,156	10.6	7,961	9.6	7,626	8.0	7,708	8.1
Non-Manufacturing	57,834	74.9	64,225	77.8	74,788	78.6	76,800	80.6
East North Central Region								
Total Employment	15,288	100.0	15,564	100.0	16,928	100.0	16,067	100.0
Manufacturing	5,054	33.0	4,603	29.4	4,655	27.5	3,968	24.7
Durables	3,604	23.6	3,285	21.0	3,314	19.6	2,710	16.9
Autos	565	3.7	541	3.5	507	3.0	475	3.0
Primary Metals	521	3.4	449	2.9	423	2.5	310	1.9
Non-Elect. Machinery	789	5.2	747	4.8	792	4.7	563	3.5
Fabricated Metals	517	3.4	506	3.2	516	3.0	435	2.7
Non-Durables	1,442	9.4	1,318	8.4	1,341	7.9	1,258	7.8
Non-Manufacturing	10,243	67.0	11,063	70.4	12,267	72.4	12,099	75.3
Michigan								
Total Employment	3,108	100.0	2,194	100.0	3,473	100.0	3,261	100.0
Manufacturing	1,072	34.5	965	30.2	988	28.4	871	26.7
Durables	855	27.5	768	24.0	784	22.6	676	20.7
Autos	345	11.1	324	10.1	315	9.1	293	9.0
Primary Metals	94	3.0	79	2.5	70	2.0	51	1.6
Non-Elect. Machinery	166	5.3	134	4.2	157	4.5	116	3.6
Fabricated Metals	120	3.9	112	3.5	110	3.2	98	3.0
Non-Durables	216	6.9	197	6.2	204	5.9	195	6.0
Non-Manufacturing	2,036	65.5	2,229	69.8	2,485	71.6	2,390	73.3

Source: Michigan Statistical Abstract Eighteenth Edition, 1984; U.S. Statistical Abstract, 104th Edition, 1984.

MICHIGAN BEYOND 2000

Table 2-2

PERCENT CHANGE IN LEVEL AND PROPORTION
OF SELECTED ECONOMIC VARIABLES
U.S., E.N.C., MICHIGAN
1970-1983

	1970	1975	1980	1983	% Change 1970-1983
Total Employment					
U.S.	77,244	82,545	95,142	95,235	23.3
E.N.C.	15,288	15,664	16,921	16,067	5.1
Michigan	3,108	3,194	3,473	3,261	4.9
E.N.C./U.S.	.198	.190	.179	.169	-14.7
MI/E.N.C.	.203	.204	.205	.203	0.0
MI/U.S.	.040	.039	.036	.034	-15.0
Manufacturing Employment					
U.S.	19,410	18,320	20,354	18,435	-5.0
E.N.C.	5,045	4,603	4,655	3,968	-21.3
MICHIGAN	1,072	965	988	871	-18.7
E.N.C./U.S.	.260	.251	.229	.215	-17.3
MI/E.N.C.	.212	.210	.212	.219	3.3
MI/U.S.	.055	.053	.049	.047	-14.5
Durables Manufacturing					
U.S.	11,254	10,694	12,226	10,727	-4.7
E.N.C.	3,604	3,285	3,314	2,710	-24.8
Michigan	855	768	784	676	-21.0
E.N.C./U.S.	.320	.307	.271	.252	-21.3
MI/E.N.C.	.237	.234	.237	.249	5.1
MI/U.S.	.076	.072	.064	.063	-17.1
Non-Durables Manufacturing					
U.S.	8,156	7,961	7,626	7,708	-5.5
E.N.C.	1,442	1,318	1,341	1,258	-12.8
Michigan	216	197	204	195	-9.7
E.N.C./U.S.	.177	.173	.165	.163	-8.0
MI/E.N.C.	.150	.149	.152	.155	3.3
MI/U.S.	.026	.025	.025	.025	-7.4

Table 2-2 (continued)

PERCENT CHANGE IN LEVEL AND PROPORTION OF SELECTED ECONOMIC VARIABLES U.S., E.N.C., MICHIGAN 1970-1983

	1970	1975	1980	1983	% Change 1970-1983
Non-Manufacturing Employment					
U.S.	57,834	64,225	74,788	76,800	32.8
E.N.C.	10,243	11,061	12,267	12,099	18.1
Michigan	2,307	2,230	2,484	2,391	17.4
E.N.C./U.S.	.177	.172	.164	.158	-10.7
MI/E.N.C.	.199	.202	.203	.197	-1.1
MI/U.S.	.035	.035	.033	.031	-11.4
Personal Income					
U.S.	803,922	1,258,642	2,156,709	2,734,121	240.0
E.N.C.	164,711	249,385	404,930	478,328	190.4
Michigan	35,975	54,540	90,703	103,980	189.0
E.N.C./U.S.	.205	.198	.188	.175	-14.6
MI/E.N.C.	.218	.219	.224	.215	-1.3
MI/U.S.	.045	.043	.042	.038	-15.5
Per Capita Personal Income					
U.S.	3,945	5,842	9,494	11,685	196.2
E.N.C.	4,085	6,067	9,709	11,517	181.9
Michigan	4,044	5,988	9,801	11,466	183.5
E.N.C./U.S.	1.035	1.039	1.023	.986	-4.7
MI/E.N.C.	.990	.987	1.009	.996	0.6
MI/U.S.	1.025	1.025	1.032	.981	-4.3
Labor Force					
U.S.	83,033	93,326	106,942	111,751	34.6
E.N.C.	16,734	18,199	19,893	20,024	19.7
Michigan	3,594	3,890	4,292	4,303	19.7
E.N.C./U.S.	.202	.195	.186	.179	-11.3
MI/E.N.C.	.215	.214	.216	.215	0.0
MI/U.S.	.043	.042	.040	.039	-9.3

Sources: Michigan Statistical Abstract, 18th Edition, 1984; U.S. Statistical Abstract, 104th Edition, 1984; Calculations by Hudson Institute.

loss was 1.1 million jobs, about 21 percent of all manufacturing employment in the five state area. The region lost employment not just to foreign countries but to other regions of the U.S. as well.[1] Had the region retained its 1970 national share of manufacturing employment in 1983, there would have been 800,000 more people at work in manufacturing industries. Some non-manufacturing employment growth did occur in the region, but at only half the rate for the U.S.. Net employment growth in all sectors was only 5.1 percent between 1970 and 1983.

Michigan demonstrated about the same pattern of employment change as the East North Central region. Manufacturing employment declined by 200,000, representing a loss of about 18 percent during the 1970-83 period. This was actually less than might have been expected based on Michigan's share of the region's manufacturing base, but again it was disproportionate in relation to national figures.

Although Michigan had somewhat more success than other North Central states in retaining manufacturing employment, non-manufacturing jobs were created at a slower rate in the state than in the region. Employment in non-manufacturing activities grew 17 percent between 1970 and 1983. Overall, employment grew by 4.9 percent despite the decline in the manufacturing sector.

Total and per capita personal income also grew more slowly in Michigan and the region than in the U.S. Total personal income in the nation grew some 240 percent from 1970 to 1983, while it increased about 190 percent in the region and the state. Since the country's population was growing while the state and the region were actually losing people, the data for per capita income do not show as marked a discrepancy. Per capita income

---

[1]According to an estimate by SRI, 45 percent of the 1972-83 job loss for this region plus Pittsburgh and Buffalo was attributable to domestic competition, 15 percent to foreign competition, 15 percent to structural change, and 25 percent to recession conditions.

grew 196 percent nationally, while in the region it grew 182 percent and in Michigan 184 percent. Per capita incomes for both the region and the state had fallen below the national average by 1983. What explains the poor performance of Michigan and the East North Central region? It is often suggested that the plants in this region are older and less efficient, and so are the first to go in a production cutback. But this reasoning does not explain the lack of investment to modernize operations within the region. It is also often suggested that this region has been the hardest hit because it is so heavily concentrated in primary metals, autos, non-electrical machinery, and other basic industries that operate in the most mature markets and against the most intense competition. While there is some truth to this contention, it does not explain, for example, why employment in the primary metals industry in the region declined less sharply than elsewhere in the nation.

A variety of factors have caused the manufacturing sector in the region to perform more poorly than in the rest of the country, but the most significant one appears to be that the cost of operating a manufacturing business in the East North Central region and in Michigan is higher than in many other areas in the country. It is worth examining this matter in more detail to illustrate some of the key issues that must be resolved if Michigan is to realize its full economic potential over the next two decades.

C. Michigan's Competitive Position

Many people in Michigan and the rest of the East North Central region are optimistic about their prospects for growth and prosperity. They believe that a region with the Midwest's concentration of financial, human, and industrial strengths cannot be "down" for long, no matter how severe the temporary setbacks it might suffer. Though there is some merit to this argument, optimism needs to be based on recognizing weaknesses as well as strengths.

Before making new investments, businesses usually go through a two step process. During the first stage potential sites for an investment are identified as providing at least a minimum level of satisfaction of needs--for example, a labor force with the minimum essential skills, or sufficient supplies of water and power. During the second stage each site that survives the initial review is ranked according to many factors that affect the costs of doing business.

The Great Lakes states, including Michigan, usually do quite well in the first stage of the evaluation. The region has an abundance of skilled workers at all levels, and the capacity to develop any skills that are not available. There is land in abundance. Most transportation needs can be met easily. The region is at the center of the largest markets in the world for both consumer goods and industrial products.

However, the region in general, and Michigan in particular, fares poorly in comparisons of location variant costs. These high costs penalize local firms that compete against those in other parts of the country or overseas. This translates into less investment by firms that might otherwise locate in the region. Ultimately, it means fewer jobs, and less economic opportunity for everyone in the region.

1. Labor Costs

The single most significant cost disadvantage for the region, and especially for Michigan, is labor cost. The total variable cost of employing a worker, including wages, employment taxes and workers' compensation insurance, is higher in Michigan than in virtually any other part of the country. While this has been true for a long time, there is evidence that the disparity is growing. In 1969 the Michigan average manufacturing wage was 124 percent of the U.S. average. By 1979 the ratio had grown to 130 percent. Although rapid growth in auto industry wages contributed to this growing gap, wages in Michigan were reported in one study to have grown faster than

U.S. wages in thirteen of seventeen industries examined.[2] A simulation study based on 1982 data determined that the cost of employing a production worker in Michigan was highest or second highest among the high-wage East North Central states in thirty-three of thirty-eight industries.[3] The differences were particularly significant in the durables industries which form the backbone of the Michigan economy. The problem is particularly acute in southeastern Michigan, but even in other parts of the state where the wage component may be more competitive, unemployment insurance and workmen's compensation costs exacerbate the differential. Since labor is the single biggest component of total business costs, this disadvantage must be remedied if Michigan's businesses are to be competitive in national or international markets. Market responses to this problem will aid in its resolution. Firms will substitute capital for labor where possible, and the lack of employment opportunities will affect the wages at which some people are willing to work. But rigidities in markets and government-imposed costs may prevent these adjustments from being rapid and complete.

2. Transportation Costs

The most significant cost advantage the region has is its location in proximity to sources of raw materials, intermediate products, and markets for its outputs. This holds true for Michigan, though its location on the northern border of the

---

[2] Johnson, George E., "Wage Rates in Michigan Compared with the Rest of the U.S." in *Michigan's Economic and Fiscal Structure*, Harvey Brazer (ed.), University of Michigan Press (Ann Arbor, 1982).

[3] Rubin, Barry M., and C. Kurt Sorn, "A Comparative Analysis of Interstate Variation in Manufacturing Business Cost: Extension to the Three Digit S.I.C. Level for the East North Central Region," School of Public and Environmental Affairs, Indiana University (1984).

region reduces that advantage to a certain extent vis-a-vis other East North Central states.[4] Many attribute the strong development of industry in the region to its central location and good transportation systems. This was no doubt true when wage differentials among states were less significant and labor costs were a smaller share of product costs.

Transportation cost remains an advantage to Michigan, but not the overwhelming one it once was. It is still of particular importance to industries whose inputs or outputs are of low value in proportion to their weight, and the investment patterns of such industries continue to reflect it.[5] However, such products tend to make up an ever smaller share of national output, and generally represent the basic industries which are suffering the most from offshore competition.

3. Energy Costs

The cost of energy is another major element in total cost. It is difficult to generalize about the relative position of Michigan or the other states in the East North Central region because so many factors influence a firm's energy costs. A firm's choice of fuel, the specifics of its production process, rates in the utility service district in which it chooses to locate, and other factors all play a role in determining actual energy costs. Michigan ranked 32nd among all states in average cost

---

[4]One disturbing element of the Saturn location decision was the expressed rationale that population (an therefore market) location shifts to the south and west make Tennessee the least cost distribution point. This explanation not only illustrates the importance of transportation costs, it also highlights the tenuousness of Michigan's current position.

[5]For example, more steel has been produced and more investments have been made by steel companies in Indiana than in any other state in the nation since around 1980.

THE COMPETITION FOR INDUSTRY

of all fuels used in manufacturing in 1980. Table 2-3 shows illustrative costs for various fuels in surrounding states.

Table 2-3

COMPARATIVE REGIONAL FUEL COSTS

	Electricity $kwh	Gas $/mcf	Coal $/ton
Indiana	3.17	2.64	35.02
Illinois	3.99	3.02	38.13
Ohio	3.11	2.90	35.35
Michigan	4.22	2.97	43.60
U.S. Average	3.31	2.65	37.36

Source: Chase Econometrics Regional Economic Data Base.

Overall, the states in the region enjoy moderate energy costs, though Michigan is at a small disadvantage compared with several neighboring states. External events such as substantial increases in the cost of imported oil or new environmental regulations concerning the burning of coal could change the relative position quickly. For example, anything that raises the cost of burning coal relative to other fuels will hurt the region's competitive position since about 90 percent of the generating capacity in the region is coal-fired, compared to 50 percent nationwide. This is an area in which the state can exert some degree of control through its regulatory policies.

The recent problems experienced with nuclear power in Michigan and elsewhere highlight the difficulty of planning for new electrical generating capacity. The Midland crisis and the effect it may yet have on Consumer's Power could have disastrous consequences for rate payers in Consumer's service area, turning a neutral cost factor into a strongly negative one. New sources of energy supplies may be considered as alternative to traditional means of increasing capacity. Several states are negotiating for supplies of hydroelectric power from Canada, which could be made available with little risk of environmental problems or price shocks.

In some states, regulators are permitting lower rates to encourage off-peak use of electric power by businesses which are highly energy intensive. This may not only reduce the need for further costly expansion of generating capacity, it could also increase total power usage and thereby reduce current costs by spreading some capital costs over a larger output. Other creative responses include mandated buy-back of cogenerated capacity, particularly in states like Michigan where there are many large manufacturing facilities using large amounts of process heat.

4. Taxation

State and local tax issues often get attention from the media, from business groups, and from public officials that is totally disproportionate to the effect these taxes have on the costs of doing business. When the deductibility of these taxes against the federal net income tax base is taken into account, they are the smallest share of total business costs. State and local taxes may affect some investment location decisions at the margin, but they are almost never significant enough to reverse the impact of the other cost disparities.

In Michigan and elsewhere there is an increasing tendency to use tax abatements or credits of various sorts to compensate for cost problems in other categories. This is generally unsound public policy because tax incentives do not alter the basic economics of an investment decision and are unfair to the rest of the tax paying public. While this type of incentive may be useful in a few special cases, it should generally be considered a tool of last resort. Property tax abatements have become so commonplace in Michigan that businesses seem to expect them as a matter of course. Yet, the State's business tax structure is not inordinately burdensome. While the subject is complex, three separate simulation studies[6] have found that the overall tax burden on businesses in Michigan is moderate. There may be equity or efficiency grounds for reforming the state's tax structure (there seems to be inordinate reliance on the property tax, for example) but the existing tax system does not appear to put Michigan businesses at a disadvantage.

D. Economic Development Policy

It is highly unlikely that government programs of promotion, financial incentives, tax abatements or other economic

---

[6]Studies by Arthur Anderson and Co. and Price-Waterhouse are cited by James E. Wheeler of the University of Michigan in "Interstate Difference in Tax Costs to Corporations," in *Michigan's Economic and Fiscal Structure*, Harvey Brazer (ed.), University of Michigan Press (Ann Arbor, 1982). The third study is the one by Robin and Zorn, cited earlier.

development activities can substantially alter investment location decisions in cases where fundamental economic factors are clearly negative. Given Michigan's large labor cost disadvantages, no state or local programs of economic development will be able to cause a "turnaround" in the state's economic fortunes. Nevertheless, government economic development policy, if well conceived, directed, and funded, can play a role in borderline cases, where the state's costs are almost competitive.

Prior to the late 1970s, most of the states in the East North Central region gave little thought to creating aggressive, intelligent, comprehensive economic development programs. Until that time the basic industries in the region were reasonably healthy and provided adequate employment growth. To the extent that economic development programs did exist, they consisted primarily of boosterism, smokestack chasing and occasional sneak raids to lure a business from a neighboring state. Incentive programs and resources differed widely from state-to-state, and even more widely from community-to-community.

Two trends emerged that forced the states to develop much more sophisticated efforts. The first was a decline in the health and growth prospects of the region's manufacturing sector. The second was the increase in the relative importance of the services sector in the national economy. These trends meant that the states in the nation's manufacturing belt could no longer depend on traditional sources of growth to provide an ever improving standard of living for growing populations. As a result, states and local governments began to look for new sources of economic growth, to devote more resources to economic development programs, and to create more sophisticated strategies for the use of those resources. They also became more aggressive in seeking out new opportunities and in competing with other jurisdictions.

Today, a business considering a major investment can pick from a menu of incentives, including low interest industrial revenue bonds, guaranteed or subsidized loans, property tax abatements, training subsidies, and a variety of other inducements. Businesses are also becoming more skilled in extracting incentives from competing governments.

1. Cost Effectiveness

The cost and effectiveness of such incentives is becoming an issue of heated debate in legislatures and council chambers. Despite the weakness of the economic and financial justification for these programs, the reality is that as long as some governments chose to compete by offering financial inducements, others feel forced to meet the competition. Michigan offers virtually the same array of inducements as other states, and it funds and uses its incentives aggressively. The state appears to be able to compete effectively for any development project it chooses.

With the increased competition and cost of economic development programs has come the recognition that limited resources must be used thoughtfully and carefully if a state or local area is to obtain the greatest return possible on its development investments. The selective emphasis is generally known as "industry targeting," in contrast to the "shotgun approach." Targeting involves such elements as selective advertising campaigns, university-based research programs (of which Michigan is said to have "almost 50"), restricted financial incentives, and personalized outreach activities. These programs have demonstrated varying degrees of success, but are usually ignored if a sufficiently tempting target of opportunity outside the selected industry presents itself.

State government and other organizations in Michigan have undertaken a number of efforts to identify target industries. A recent report from the Southeast Michigan Council of Governments identified at least eight "readily available studies" that tagged some sixty possible target industries from minemouth gasifiers to ethnic foods. Even if it were possible to develop effective programs to target sixty industries, the greatest hope for prosperity in Michigan is the auto industry and the traditional and nascent industries that support it. While targeting new non-automotive ventures may be a good idea, Michigan must not overlook its obvious target.

Most economic growth comes from the creation or expansion of firms in an area. Studies have found that the number of jobs created by firms moving into an area is only about one-sixth of the total of all jobs created in that area. As a result, many states are beginning to put more time and resources into incentives designed to promote investments by existing firms. Some states are also beginning to work with local entrepreneurs in order to promote the creation of new enterprises. Programs directed toward existing businesses seem to be generating good returns on the resources invested.

A few states have begun to examine the possibility of promoting the development of service businesses. These states are generally limiting their efforts to services that might be regarded as part of the state's "export base" (e.g., financial services, advertising, or in some circumstances even health care).[7] Even with this limited focus, these states that are attempting to become involved with the services sector are having difficulty. Traditional economic development incentives work poorly for services businesses because those programs are generally oriented toward providing financing for fixed assets, while the most important requirement for services businesses is low-cost working capital. Other problems include the riskiness and limited growth prospects of most service businesses. This does not appear to be a promising area for economic developers, and Michigan's lack of emphasis on this sector is probably wise.

The alternative to promoting services with tools designed to promote manufacturing is to develop tools appropriate to the

---

[7]This is in keeping with the premise on which traditional industrial development programs are usually based: that only those activities that generate sales outside the area can bring additional income into it. Thus, it has been goods-producing businesses that export their products from an area that have been the focus of most economic development activities.

task. The most advantageous way for Michigan to develop its service industries is probably to identify a few service businesses that have the potential to play a particularly central role in the state and to develop specific programs to nurture them. For example, if the service businesses involved in "paperless" manufacturing are expected to be important to the survival of the state's manufacturing sector, then programs should be developed to promote that industry. For example, a program of loans for Michigan students in appropriate fields of study could be developed, with a portion of the loan forgiven for each year the student remains in Michigan working in that field. Similarly, the state could provide subsidized tuition relief for employees of firms in specific industries. In these ways, the state could subsidize the cost of the human capital that is usually so crucial to service businesses much as it subsidizes physical capital for manufacturers.

2. The Local Role

A final aspect of the changing nature of economic development in the region is the growing participation of local communities. In the early 1970s only a few of the largest cities in the region had organized economic development programs; now communities with populations as small as 20,000 often have a full-time economic developer and sometimes even an advertising budget. Some Michigan cities have sophisticated economic development programs, for example, Battle Creek's use of a foreign trade sub-zone as the focal point of a program to bring foreign investment into the area. In other cities economic development activities are rudimentary or non-existent. Most cities have only a very limited identification with and commitment to state government's economic development efforts. As other state governments in the region have done, Michigan should make a concerted effort to enhance its position as coordinator and leader in economic development matters throughout the state.

MICHIGAN BEYOND 2000

E. New Industrial Possibilities

Michigan's economic fate over the next twenty years will hinge largely on the success of its auto industry. This success may depend partly on the development of a variety of new technologies and products. Some of these new technologies may spawn entirely new industries that will play important roles in the state's economic future. These industries may be of special significance to Michigan because its cost disadvantages are less important for them than is the case with mature industries. Other factors such as proximity to markets, access to capital, or the location of research activities may largely determine the investment decisions made by firms in these industries, as was the case with the auto industry at the beginning of the century.

Since virtually all new products and industries depend to some degree on the development of new technologies, any forecast of new industrial possibilities is highly speculative. This section of the study focuses on the development and commercialization of a few technologies that are already beginning to make their presence felt, and that might play key roles in Michigan's economic future.

1. Robotics

The most exciting near-term prospect, and the one which may have the greatest overall impact on the state's economy, is robotics. Robotics is not a single technology. It includes a variety of technologies that enable a machine to sense its external environment, to make decisions based on sensory inputs, and to execute its decisions with speed and precision. These technologies include cybernetics and artificial intelligence; machine vision, tactile, and other sensor technologies; hydraulics, mechanical and electrical engineering; and electronics. Technological advances that contribute to the advancement of robotics products are taking place regularly but somewhat unevenly in all of these fields. With each advance, new applications for robotic devices are created.

THE COMPETITION FOR INDUSTRY

There are great similarities between the robotics industry of today and the computer industry of twenty-five years ago. As is the case with today's robots, the computers of 1960 were large, ungainly, inflexible, expensive, best suited to a limited number of repetitive tasks, and employed almost exclusively by government and very large businesses. The desk top computers of 1985 are faster, more flexible and have more capabilities than their 1960s predecessors at about one one-thousandth the cost. Twenty years from now robotic devices may well have experienced similar technological evolution and price declines. They may become as ubiquitous on the plant floor as computers are in the office, and may have begun to insinuate themselves into homes.

This provides an exciting prospect for Michigan if it can sustain a leadership role in robotics technologies and production. In the near-term, robotics and other advanced automation techniques will be crucial to the fate of the auto industry and other basic industries in Michigan. In the longer-term, these industries may be just as important to the state as the computer industry was in New York, Massachusetts, Texas and California.

2. Biological Sciences

Another set of developing technologies that holds out exciting possibilities for Michigan is related to biological sciences. These technologies may be more important in their application than in their development. Two, in the field of genetic engineering, may have particular importance to this state.

The overall situation in agriculture in Michigan is not good. Farm output in physical units and cash value has increased substantially in the last thirty years, but inflation-adjusted net farm income has fallen dramatically. A major cause of this trend has been farming practices that are intended to maximize yield. Little attention has been paid to the cost of inputs such as fertilizer, fuel, insecticides and herbicides, and capital equipment. As farming has become more input-intensive, as inputs have become more expensive, and as commodity prices have softened, the effect on farm income has been devastating. Genetic engineering of new strains of crops and even animals make it possible that in a few years the basic philosophy of farming will change from one of maximizing total output to one of maximizing output per unit of input. This could do a great deal for the finances of farmers. It should put much less stress on the land and environment, and it should require the use of fewer valuable resources in the production of food.

Another interesting possibility is the development of biological agents that could be used to generate chemical reactions. At present, most complex chemical reactions, particularly those involving organic compounds, require high temperatures and pressures. Several such reactions must be used in the production of many plastic and synthetic fibers products from wood feedstocks, for example. These processes are expensive because they require large amounts of energy and complex capital equipment. It is conceivable that unicellular organisms could be developed that would produce organic chemical feedstocks directly from the cellulose found in wood, farm waste and other organic products, and do so at ambient temperature and pressure. This would reduce the energy and capital costs involved in producing feedstocks and it would create an industry which is highly sensitive to the transportation costs of raw materials. The result could be a new generation of environmentally sound chemical production facilities springing up in the forests of Northern Michigan.

F. Michigan's Economic Future

Among the major factors that will influence the evolution of Michigan's economy over the next twenty years are:

- o   The transition to post-industrial economies among the advanced nations and the industrialization of many of the less developed countries.
- o   The recovery and "reindustrialization" of the domestic auto industry.

THE COMPETITION FOR INDUSTRY

o   The interregional shifts in population and economic activity in the U.S.
o   The trend in Michigan's comparative advantage vis-a-vis other states in the region and the U.S.
o   New technologies and the development of new products and manufacturing processes.

The range of possible economic futures for Michigan is incredibly wide because these factors and many others, both internal and external, play important, if not always well understood, roles. This section presents one possible economic outcome for Michigan developed within the context of relatively optimistic assumptions concerning the U.S. economy.

This scenario assumes that Michigan is operating in a national economic environment characterized by:

o   Population reaching approximately 275 million by 2005.
o   3.0 - 3.5 percent average annual rate of growth in Gross National Product.
o   1.5 - 2.0 percent average annual rate of growth in labor productivity.
o   Gradual downward adjustment of the value of the dollar to exchange rates (particularly vis-a-vis the yen) consonant with purchasing power parity.
o   The absence of severe new restrictions on international trade flows.

In this context, several factors are of particular importance to Michigan. Foremost is the ability of the auto industry to remain competitive against a growing array of foreign producers, and the ability of the state to retain or even expand its share of auto production. To a major extent this will depend on the ability of the state to become a center of advanced manufacturing technology, and the success of the auto industry in applying that technology. It is difficult to conceive of other industries or activities that could fully take up the economic slack that would be created by even a moderately widespread failure in the state's manufacturing sector to achieve technological leadership.

Michigan must also have "good luck and good management" to resolve a number of special issues that confront the state:

- o Labor cost differentials vis-a-vis other states must be reduced and ultimately eliminated.
- o Other labor costs (e.g., workmen's compensation and unemployment insurance) must be brought into line.
- o Environmentally sound hazardous waste management practices adequate to support continued high levels of industrial activity must be implemented.
- o State government must improve the state's fiscal management practices.

These are complex and difficult issues that will require creativity, effort, and the cooperation of numerous entities to resolve them. The resolution of some of these issues will not benefit every citizen of Michigan. For example, the reduction of labor cost differentials will initially reduce the incomes of some workers. It is conceivable that retail sales growth could be somewhat slower than otherwise, at least until the number employed rises in response to wage adjustments. These adjustments are inevitable, but the negative consequences can be mitigated. For example, if union wage demands were held below the combined rate of productivity increases and inflation the wage adjustment process could occur without the givebacks that were necessary in some industries during the last recession. Should such concessions be traded for employment guarantees, the state would experience both a relatively painless wage adjustment and more stable employment than otherwise. More contentious approaches to resolving this issue would probably result in less stable employment, and reduced prospects for the state to retain a successful manufacturing sector.

The probable result of two decades of moderately good management and good luck in Michigan, particularly among the auto industry and its suppliers, is a state that is less dependent on manufacturing, less affected by recession, but somewhat less well off relative to the rest of the nation.

Michigan will still be home to slightly more than nine million people in 2005. Relatively higher rates of population growth in other areas of the country will result in Michigan's share of total U.S. population dropping to about 3.3 percent, approximately what it was before the massive industrialization of the state in the early years of the twentieth century. This will come about in large part because the state will have relatively few new high wage jobs as employment in manufacturing declines and employment grows in services, and wholesale and retail trade. This shift in employment mix will result in relatively high out-migration, particularly of the educated young seeking better employment opportunities.

Nonetheless, Michigan residents will be substantially wealthier in 2005 than they are now. Real per capita personal income will grow to almost double the 1980 level, buoyed by relatively high rates of economic expansion nation-wide. Productivity increases will average about two percent per year, spread over a wide variety of economic sectors. They will largely be the result of increased use of more automated equipment in the production of goods, and the spread of highly sophisticated information and communications systems in the services sector.

In relation to the rest of the U.S., however, Michigan residents will not be as well off. Because much of Michigan's manufacturing activity is concentrated in low growth industries that are under pressure to install ever more automated production technologies, employment in high wage manufacturing jobs will show virtually no increase; in fact, it will show a slight reduction from the peak it reached just after World War II (not quite 1.2 million jobs). Much of the job growth that does take place in Michigan will be in the retail and personal service sectors, which traditionally pay lower wages, while other parts of the country that industrialized later and host faster growing industries will see at least moderate growth in manufacturing employment. Wages paid in the auto industry will decline relative to other wages, and the overall wage structure in

Michigan will come into closer conformity with other areas. As a result, per capita personal income in Michigan will be slightly below the U.S. average.

Employment will remain more concentrated in manufacturing in Michigan that it is elsewhere. The composition of manufacturing employment, however, is likely to change dramatically (see Table 2-4). The auto industry will employ about 50 percent fewer people in Michigan than it did at its postwar peak, with most of the employment losses coming in direct production jobs. Michigan's share of total U.S. motor vehicle production of about 11 million units will have remained at about one third. The reductions in production employment will be made possible by increased use of advanced flexible automation equipment that will require fewer direct labor hours needed for the construction of a vehicle. Automation will also change the nature of the work done by production employees. Virtually all of the dangerous or highly routine work will be done by machine, as will most material handling. Workers will be concentrated in process control, statistical quality control, maintenance, and other non-routine activities.

Employment in other industries comprising the auto complex will not show declines of the same magnitude. In fact, employment in the automation industry (now known as non-electrical machinery) can be expected to increase as the equipment it produces begins to find applications in stores, offices, warehouses, and homes. Employment in this segment of the industry could grow enough to more than offset the losses experienced in the manufacture of more traditional machines and tools. Similarly, employment in the production of non-metal materials may grow enough to offset declines in employment in the primary metals industry, which will see significant improvements in product, process, and levels of productivity, but not employment growth.

Other industries which can be expected to demonstrate increased levels of employment over 1980 are food products, chemicals, lumber and wood products, and perhaps paper manufacturing. Almost all net employment growth will occur in the non-manufacturing sector, which can be expected to grow at

Table 2-4

SELECTED SOCIO-ECONOMIC VARIABLES FOR MICHIGAN 1980 AND 2005, OPTIMISTIC SCENARIO

	1980	2005
Population		
Total	9,262,000	9,150,000
As % of U.S.	4.1	3.3
Personal Income (1980 Dollars)		
Total (in Million)	91,363	165,800
As % of U.S.	4.23	3.25
Per Capita	9,872	18,120
As % of U.S.	103.8	98.5
Labor Force	4,290,000	4,950,000
Employment		
Total	3,442,800	4,676,000
Manufacturing	998,900	1,035,000
Automotive	326,300	200,000
Non-Manufacturing	2,443,900	3,641,000
Manufacturing as % of Total	29.0%	22.8%
Unemployment Rate	12.4	5.5

Source: U.S. Census Bureau, Michigan Department of Commerce, Hudson Institute.

about 1.5 percent per year. The highest rate of growth and the greatest number of new jobs will occur in the services sector, particularly personal services such as travel and tourism, and health care. Other segments of the non-manufacturing sector which are likely to experience significant increases in employment are retail trade and communications. Increases in government employment at the state and local level can also be expected, resulting from the combined effects of an increase in the social surplus which supports government activities, rising expectations concerning the level of services to be provided by government, and a continued trend toward provision of those services by state and local agencies.

The most promising feature of the figures in Table 2-5 is the low unemployment rate they imply. The growth in income and employment coupled with a virtually stable population will reduce the structural unemployment problem in Michigan even in the face of a labor force which is expected to grow at about 0.5 percent annually. The lessened influence of the manufacturing sector in the state's economy should also reduce the problem of cyclical swings.

1. The Downside Risks

There are a variety of factors, at both the national and state levels, that could produce less sanguine results that those just discussed.

It is easiest to imagine circumstances in which Michigan's auto complex is competitively unsuccessful. Forces outside Michigan, such as a series of deep and prolonged national recessions, could reduce the growth in demand for automobiles. Severe protectionist legislation could induce more Japanese investment in auto production facilities in the U.S. outside of Michigan, with U.S. producers following. If the industry does not make the investment required to update its production processes, if the labor/management issues involved in the transition prove intractable, or if automation technology does not advance as expected, the Japanese and others could control

THE COMPETITION FOR INDUSTRY

Table 2-5

ESTIMATED DISTRIBUTION OF MICHIGAN EMPLOYMENT IN 2005 BY SECTOR (THOUSANDS)

Manufacturing	1,035
Durables	760
Metals	125
Non-Electrical Machinery	200
Electrical Machinery	85
Transportation Equipment	220
Motor Vehicles	200
Other	20
Other Durable Goods	130
Non-Durables	275
Food Products	65
Textiles	20
Paper and Allied Products	35
Printing and Publishing	35
Chemicals, Petroleum and Related Products	70
Other Non-Durable Goods	50
Private Non-Manufacturing Industries	2,910
Contract Construction	125
Trans., Communications, and Public Utilities	230
Wholesale Trade	265
Retail Trade	830
Finance, Insurance, Real Estate	215
Services	1,275
Government	700

Source: Hudson Institute.

a much larger share of the domestic market than their projected 35 percent.

Should that happen the effects in Michigan would be devastating. Direct employment in the auto industry could drop as low as 100,000, with most of those remaining employed in non-production activities. With similar employment reductions in auto-related industries, Michigan's manufacturing employment could easily fall to 750,000 or less.

Total and per capita personal income would grow much more slowly than forecast in the optimistic scenario, though natural growth in productivity would still generate substantial improvement. This growth in income would produce growth in employment in services and trade, but as many as 750,000 fewer jobs would be created compared to the more sanguine circumstance outlined earlier.

This scarcity of jobs, particularly high-paying manufacturing jobs, could lead to net out-migration at a pace similar to that experienced by the state in the early 1980s. The result of such out-migration could be a decline in total population of at least a million people. The modest increase in total employment would be more than outstripped by increases in the labor force, with two worker families becoming even more the norm as families attempt to maintain living standards in the face of employment losses or income declines. An increase in structural unemployment to levels as high as those experienced previously only in major recessions would not be surprising.

Chapter 3
A CLOSE LOOK AT THE AUTOMOBILE INDUSTRY

The overriding importance of the auto industry to Michigan's future justifies a more detailed look at this critical industry.

Where does this industry stand today? What are the major forces that have shaped it over the last two decades, and what do these trends mean for the state of Michigan?

Without question the most important development of the past two decades--and one that continues to dominate the industry today--is the challenge from Japan. The decade long emergence of Japanese producers as the leaders in auto manufacturing has triggered far-reaching changes in American production management, labor relations, and supplier organizations. All of these changes have major consequences for Michigan.

A. The Japanese Challenge

Over the past two decades the import share of total vehicle sales has risen steadily, from 5 percent in 1965 to 21 percent in 1984 (Figure 3-1). The increase in Japanese share has been even more spectacular: while Japan supplied only .3 percent of all vehicles sold in the U.S. in 1965, they captured 17.3 percent in 1984. Two decades ago it was the challenge of the low priced Volkswagen Beetle that concerned the American

MICHIGAN BEYOND 2000

Figure 3-1

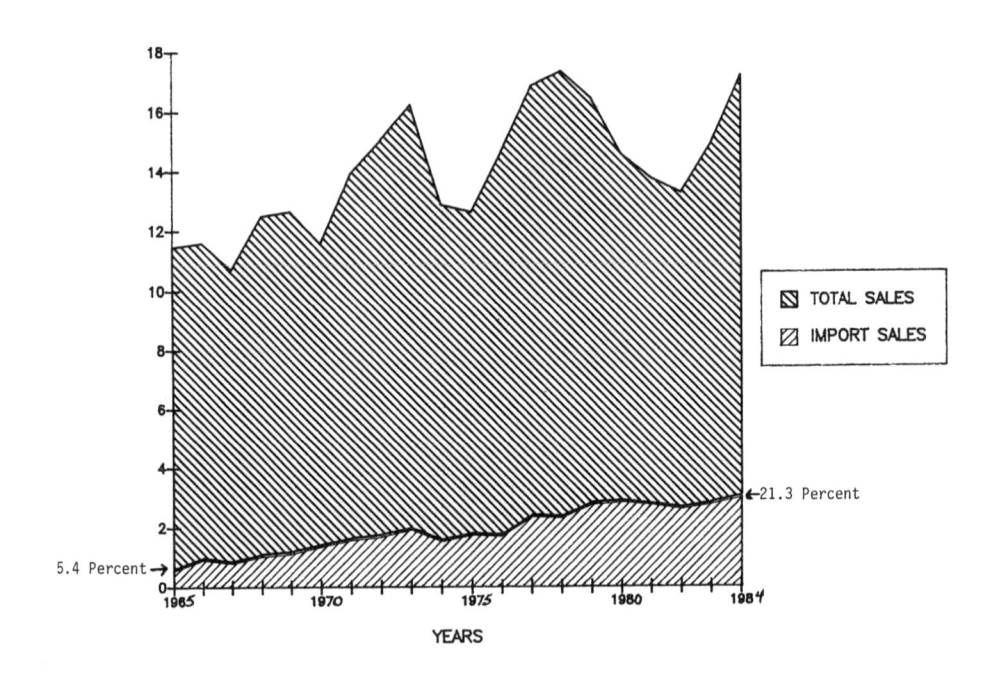

IMPORTS TO THE U.S. MARKET HAVE GROWN
RAPIDLY OVER THE PAST TWO DECADES

Source: Arvid Jouppa Associates, *Jama Forum*, Volume 3, No. 4.

A CLOSE LOOK AT THE AUTOMOBILE INDUSTRY

auto industry. Today 83 percent of all imports come from Japan.

The reasons for this erosion of American market share have been widely analyzed and reported. First, of course, is the highly publicized gap in manufacturing efficiency between Japan and the United States. While estimates vary, analysts both in and out of the auto industry believe that Japanese producers can deliver cars to the United States at a cost that is $1500 to $2500 cheaper than domestically produced models, even after paying approximately $500 in freight and duties. Perhaps 30-40 percent of this difference may be a reflection of currency rates (a perennially undervalued yen and a recently overvalued dollar). But much of it reflects a real economic advantage enjoyed by the Japanese producers.

For example, a 1981 study done for the U.S. Department of Transportation indicated that Japanese companies could assemble a car using approximately 80 hours of total labor, compared with an average of 130 for domestic makers.[1] Japanese plants reportedly use one-third as much space as typical American plants, and carry one-tenth as much in-process inventory.

Wage rates are also higher in the U.S. auto industry than in Japan, with current hourly labor costs averaging about $23 per hour, compared to about $14 in Japan.[2] Another study noted that white collar salaries are also part of the problem, with the average salary of U.S. chief executives, excluding bonuses and stock options, 12 to 18 times the income of the highest paid blue collar worker, compared to a ratio of 6 to 8 times in Japanese companies.[3] Another report estimated that

---

[1] Jim Harbour and William Abernathy, Harvard University Business School, D.O.T Contract No. 6117.

[2] "Can Detroit Cope This Time?" *Business Week*, April 22, 1985.

[3] Vladimir Pucik, "White Collar Human Resource Management: A Comparison of the U.S. and Japanese Automobile Industries," *Columbia Journal of World Business*, Fall 1984, p. 93.

white collar wages contributed 48 percent to the labor cost differential between Japanese and U.S. firms.[4]

In addition to the problems of cost, Japanese automobiles enjoy apparent quality advantages. As judged by surveys of new car buyers and frequency of repair data collected by consumer organizations, Japanese models are rated more highly than American ones in almost every size and class of vehicle. for example, of 216 foreign and domestic cars reviewed by *Consumer Reports* magazine in April of 1985, 78 percent of recent American models scored "worse than average" or "much worse than average" in frequency of repair ratings. Ninety-six percent of Japanese models achieved "better than average" or "much better than average" scores.

B. The American Response

In order to survive, American manufacturers have undertaken an unprecedented effort to improve their competitive position. While the mix of strategies varies among the major companies, each is employing three main approaches : (1) dramatically improve the efficiency of U.S. factories; (2) re-orient supplier relationships to rely more on lower cost domestic or foreign suppliers; and (3) shift the mix of U.S. production upscale, conceding the small car market to foreign suppliers.

By adopting methods learned (or relearned) from Japanese producers, American automakers plan to dramatically cut the costs of U.S. production. By rearranging production, grouping suppliers nearby, investing more heavily in automation, and rewriting work rules, domestic manufacturers hope to make giant improvements in their production cost. For example, the revamping of GM's Buick facilities in Flint will enable the company to produce an equivalent number of cars in 1986 with 40 percent fewer workers than were required last year. Even greater gains may lie ahead. GM's Saturn program has targeted

---

[4]M.S. Flynn, "Compensation Levels and Systems," Joint U.S.-Japan Automotive Study, Working Paper Series No. 21, University of Michigan, 1984 (Part III).

A CLOSE LOOK AT THE AUTOMOBILE INDUSTRY

a 50 percent or greater reduction in direct manufacturing labor for its new line of vehicles. Both Ford and Chrysler have similar programs that aim to achieve substantial labor cost reductions.

Along with these efforts comes an acceleration of programs to shift parts production to lower cost suppliers. In some cases, this involves new supplier relationships, such as concentrating multi-year orders among a few of the lowest cost, highest quality suppliers. In others it means shifting production overseas. Many parts traditionally purchased by the large automakers, such as brakes and fuel systems, are increasingly likely to be made overseas in order to save costs or satisfy foreign production requirements. General Motors, Ford, and Chrysler have all accelerated efforts to source more parts from Mexico, Brazil, and the Pacific Basin countries.

Because they represent such a large fraction of the value of each car, the costs of engines and drivetrains are of particular importance. Among the "Big Three," these major mechanicals have historically been supplied from wholly owned, domestic plants. In recent years, Mexico has become a source of engines for U.S. automakers, and it is likely that this trend will continue. According to internal company estimates, Mexico and Korea offer a 10 percent to 30 percent cost advantage compared with domestic production.

The final and most recently adopted American strategy has been to concede the U.S. small car market to the Japanese and to concentrate domestic production on compact and larger cars. General Motors has arranged to import vehicles from Suzuki and Isuzu, and will jointly manufacture a car designed by Toyota in Fremont, California. Ford, working with Mazda, and Chrysler with Mitsubishi are adopting similar strategies. Within the next few years, these captive imports will supply most of the subcompact cars sold by U.S. producers.

C. The Next Wave

The challenge to traditional American manufacturers is likely to be extended in the near future by two other developments: the rapid growth of domestic U.S. production by

MICHIGAN BEYOND 2000

Japanese automakers, and the potential for significant imports from other low wage countries such as Korea, Spain, and Yugoslavia.

Since 1980, when Volkswagen established a plant in New Stanton, Pennsylvania, production by foreign manufacturers in the U.S. has grown by more than 150 percent, reaching 440,000 units in 1984. By 1990, when facilities owned by Honda, Nissan, Toyota-GM, Toyota, Mazda, and Mitsubishi are in full operation, more than 1,000,000 units a year will be produced in foreign-owned domestic facilities.

Because these plants produce cars designed and engineered outside the U.S., and typically rely on foreign plants for supplies of their major components, they create fewer U.S. jobs and have potentially lower cost structures than traditional U.S. plants. And because most of these facilities are located outside Michigan, they represent a potential drain on the Michigan economy to the extent they replace Michigan plants.

In addition to domestic production in foreign-owned plants, new challenges are possible from producers in other low wage countries, particularly Korea. Last year, Hyundai, a major Korean automaker, began exports to Canada, becoming the largest single exporter of vehicles to the country in less than 12 months. Producers based in Spain and Yugoslavia have undertaken or announced similar plans to export to North America. Although vehicles produced in these countries many not be fully competitive in quality with the U.S. standard, much less the Japanese, they could become so as these economies mature, particularly in the low end of the vehicle market.

Additional joint ventures between American and Japanese companies and foreign producers (e.g., Hyundai/Mitsubishi, GM/Daewoo, Chrysler/Samsung) could rapidly accelerate introduction of vehicles from these countries. By providing ready access to the American market through established dealer networks and building on the reputations, guarantees, and parts supply systems of established makers, production from such joint ventures could escalate rapidly.

A CLOSE LOOK AT THE AUTOMOBILE INDUSTRY

D. Michigan's Share of Production

Even if U.S. automakers succeed in turning back the tide of imports, Michigan still faces a considerable challenge in maintaining its historic position as the dominant producer of U.S. automobiles and auto parts. Over the last 20 years, Michigan's share of U.S. motor vehicle production has remained stable at about 33 percent while its share of employment has fallen only slightly:

Michigan's Share of U.S. Auto
Production and Employment
(Percent)

	1965	1970	1975	1980	1983
Auto Production	35	32	33	27	30
Truck Production	27	26	33	27	29
Employment	43	42	41	41	39

Source: *Michigan Statistical Abstract, 1984.*

This stability is a reflection of historic advantages that Michigan has enjoyed: the combination of existing plants, a skilled workforce, a supplier network in place, and native sons in charge of decisionmaking. Offsetting these advantages in recent years has been a growing wage rate disadvantage, coupled with higher associated costs for workers' compensation, unemployment insurance, and health care.

During the industry's first 50 years, automobile plants were largely located according to serendipity and accident. Many of the industry's founders lived in Michigan and new facilities were often simply sited near the original ones for convenience. Even after the ascendance of modern corporate decisionmaking, this pattern, as well as corporate sensitivity to the economic impacts of plant closings, often led to decisions to locate in Michigan whether or not it was strictly the lowest cost location.

Today the competitive environment virtually forces selection of the lowest cost alternative. While Michigan enjoys obvious advantages because of its existing infrastructure, a growing fraction of automobile employment--for research and development, marketing, and other management functions--is not directly tied to the location of production. In addition, some of Michigan's advantages are waning. For example, the benefits of a skilled labor force are declining as the auto industry automates. While many of the skills of existing employees can be transferred or upgraded (for example, in electrical and mechanical maintenance), some of the jobs being added (programmers, electronics engineers, systems analysts) are not ones in which Michigan has an advantage.

Michigan's dense network of suppliers is certainly still important, but it is an advantage that can apparently be transplanted, or shipped as product. The clustering of new supplier plants near the Nissan assembly facility in Smyrna, Tennessee, for example, suggests that relocation of suppliers can occur relatively quickly. And the interstate highway network means that supplier plants throughout the upper Midwest are equally accessible to assembly facilities in several states.

"Just-in-time" production--the system pioneered by the Japanese that clusters suppliers near the point of final assembly and reduces in-process inventory as much as possible--will also have a profound impact on Michigan's future. There is now little doubt that maximum efficiency requires minimum in-process inventory, and that nearby sources of supply are key to achieving these gains. As a result, the location of final assembly operations will have an even greater impact than it has historically on the development of auxiliary and supporting industries. Currently, Michigan has 14 major assembly facilities. Only if these facilities remain in the state will just-in-time production benefit Michigan.

The recent decision by Mazda to locate a U.S. assembly facility in Flat Rock, Michigan, is an encouraging sign, especially since it was the first such decision by a foreign automaker to locate in the state. Similarly, recent decisions by GM and Ford to make heavy new investments in Michigan are hopeful signs.

But the decision to site the new GM Saturn plant in Spring Hill, Tennessee does not augur well. Because Saturn is considered so central to GM's future as a U.S. producer (and is

A CLOSE LOOK AT THE AUTOMOBILE INDUSTRY

likely to be emulated by other U.S. producers) its decision to locate the facility outside the state is particularly ominous.

In the Saturn case, the company's objective was to strip away as much of the accumulated corporate fat as possible, and to begin with a "clean sheet of paper." Every facet of corporate practice--wage scales, job assignments, the arrangement of work flow, pay practices, supplier relationships, even dealer relationships--was scrutinized to redefine the most efficient production technique. Southeastern Michigan, with its high wage scales, its history of combative labor relationships, its heavily union influenced government bureaucracies, and its high health, welfare, and workers' compensation costs was perceived by the company to be part of the manufacturing cost problem, not as a location for its solution. To the extent that Saturn succeeds in setting a new standard of U.S. production efficiency, Michigan will be a major loser, as GM and other automakers emulate this new prototype.

Of course, it is possible that the Saturn experience will be adapted to Michigan as new investments are made over the next two decades. Kalamazoo was reported to be one of the finalists in the competition for the Saturn plant. But new investment in radically modernized plants is not certain, given the industry's obvious need to change fundamentally in order to become competitive. If the perception develops that the industry can become competitive only by leaving Michigan, the state would lose its share of production quickly.

Competitive dynamics will also affect the state. Michigan is the state of GM, Ford, and Chrysler. If any of these three lose market share to foreign producers or to the new producers who have located outside the state, Michigan will suffer.

E. Auto Production in Michigan--The Next Twenty Years

Over the next two decades, Michigan's automobile industry will be affected by five major trends: (1) slow but steady growth in new car sales; (2) rapidly rising productivity; (3) continued loss of market share to imports; (4) an increase in

U.S. production by Japanese producers; and (5) a significant upscaling in the price and features of U.S. produced cars.

The first and last of these trends should have positive impacts on auto employment in Michigan. These favorable trends are likely to be far outweighed, however, by the combined impacts of productivity gains and increased competition from on- and off-shore production by foreign auto manufacturers. In combination, these unfavorable factors are likely to shrink automotive employment significantly in Michigan, particularly among production workers. By 2005, total automotive employment in Michigan is likely to fall by almost 50 percent, to only 200,000 workers, while production employment may slip as low as 120,000 workers.

1. The Demand for Motor Vehicles

Despite predictions of stagnating or declining motor vehicles sales as a result of rising energy prices or saturation of the markets, the U.S. car and truck market should continue to grow over the next two decades, although the rate of gain may fall below the pace of the 1960s and 1970s.

The most important factor helping to boost auto sales will be continued growth of personal income. Throughout the last 20 years, motor vehicles have been a remarkably stable proportion of personal consumption expenditures. In 1960, for example, the auto share of personal spending stood at 6.1 percent, compared to 6.5 percent in 1984. With incomes predicted nearly to double between 1980 and 2005, auto sales are likely to climb by a similar proportion.

Demographics will also play a part. By the year 2005, the driving age population will climb by about 14 percent. Since 1970, the ratio of vehicles to licensed drivers has increased steadily, from .96 to 1.06. If this ratio continues to edge upward, while the number of drivers climbs with the pace of population growth, total vehicle registrations should grow by 25 percent. Combined with replacement demand, this growth should push new car and truck sales up by an average of 1-1.5 percent per year, reaching approximately 16-19 million units annually by 2005.

A CLOSE LOOK AT THE AUTOMOBILE INDUSTRY

A number of factors could reduce this total, including slower economic growth, shifts in spending priorities, or a new spurt in the price of oil. On the other hand, improvements in vehicles, such as new, lighter materials, sophisticated electronic controls, or advanced transmissions and engines could accelerate the replacement cycle for vehicles, increasing sales. For example, by the turn of the century, vehicles with high temperature engines, continuously variable transmissions, and high strength plastic bodies, may be available. Advancements such as these, or simply new versions of old ideas--e.g., the recent revival of the minivan--could push auto sales above the predicted rate.

2. Productivity Growth

During the period from 1955 to 1978, automotive industry labor productivity--the number of cars produced by each worker each year--grew by an average of 3.1 percent annually, doubling the output per worker. Although recessions cut productivity gains during the 1980s, productivity rebounded sharply in 1983 and 1984, leaping by an estimated 21 percent.

Over the next two decades, productivity is likely to increase at least as fast as it has over the past two. Reforms in inventory control (e.g., just-in-time production), the organization of production (e.g., locating stamping plants next to assembly facilities), and labor-management relations (e.g., reducing the numbers of job classifications and work rules) are likely to have major impacts on productivity within the next 5-8 years. After that, plants are likely to become increasingly automated, as advances in machine vision and robot controls allow machines to perform a greater variety of assembly tasks, and as the price of robots continues to fall. By the year 2000, the best automobile assembly plants may resemble today's highly automated chemical plants, with relatively few employees monitoring and repairing huge complexes of tools and equipment.

Although these productivity gains could be slowed by recessions, financial constraints, or labor disagreements, it is likely that productivity in the future will advance at least as fast as its recent historic trend. If this occurs, it will be possible by the year 2005 to make the same number of cars with half the number of production workers employed today.

3. The Growth of Imports

Between 1965 and 1984, Japanese exports to the United State have risen at a rate of 9 percent compounded annually. If the twenty year rate of growth of Japanese imports were to continue unabated over the next twenty years, the Japanese would own some 95 percent of the American automobile industry by the year 2005. Although such spectacular, unchecked growth is possible, it is much more likely that economic or political factors will intervene to slow the growth of imports.

In the short-term, export quotas imposed by the Japanese government are likely to curb expansion of car imports, while high U.S. tariffs will continue to hold down light truck imports (since 1980, the U.S. has imposed a 25 percent tariff on light trucks entering the country from Japan).

Over the longer-term it is possible that improving American productivity, gradually narrowing wage differentials between U.S. and Japanese workers and executives, and a realignment of the relationship between the Japanese yen and the American dollar will narrow the gap between U.S. and Japanese production costs. If these trends do occur, they would tend to slow the growth of Japanese imports in the years after 1990.

If the manufacturing cost gap does not fade, it is likely that political restrictions will be continued. Given the export oriented structure of the Japanese economy, trade frictions between the U.S. and Japan are likely to be sustained indefinitely. If the Japanese do not respond to American concerns, some legislated or negotiated restrictions on automobiles are almost sure to be re-imposed by the U.S. as they were during 1980.

In either case, Japanese auto imports will not rise as fast as history and current economics imply. A third factor will tend to reinforce this slower growth: the widespread perception that U.S. imports will continue to be restricted. In order to supply even 50 percent of the American market, the Japanese would have to add the capacity to produce 6 million new cars in

A CLOSE LOOK AT THE AUTOMOBILE INDUSTRY

Japan. Given the uncertainties regarding the long-term political environment for trade, the potential competitiveness of highly automated American production facilities, and the recent government promoted increase in the value of the yen, the huge investments necessary to create this production capacity are likely to be viewed very cautiously in Japan, particularly by the largest producers such as Toyota and Nissan. If the large producers indefinitely delay major additions to their auto production capacity because of fears about their ability to market these cars in America, these fears will become self-fulfilling prophecies, as capacity constraints lead to lower sales.

These factors make it realistic to assume that Japanese car and truck imports will grow more slowly--at perhaps half their historic rate--during the period from 1990 to 2005. This slower growth, coupled with an increasing total market, would result in imports holding only about a third of the U.S. market by the year 2005.

4. Increased U.S. Production by Foreign Automakers

In response to trade restraints and threats, Japanese producers are likely to establish and expand automobile production facilities in the United States. Currently Honda, Nissan, Toyota, Mazda and Mitsubishi have built or announced their intentions to build U.S. domestic facilities, in addition to Renault (AMC) and Volkswagen, who also have U.S. production facilities.

Typically, assembly plants are designed to produce 240,000 to 300,000 units annually, suggesting that if all seven foreign producers fully utilized their plants they could deliver approximately 1.5-2.0 million vehicles annually to the U.S. market. In practice, it is unlikely that all of the units will produce at capacity, and uncertain whether all will remain in operation. For example, Renault and Volkswagen have experienced difficulties and may not remain U.S. producers indefinitely. Despite these uncertainties, it is likely that production at these facilities will increase dramatically over the next 5-8 years, reaching 1 million by the early 1990s.

After 1990, further increases will depend greatly on the trade environment, and the relative competitive position of U.S. and Japanese production locations. While some further gains in domestic production by foreign automakers are likely, these increases may not match the near-term growth, unless stricter import restraints are imposed. If imports continue to climb in the 1990s, intense competition in the small and medium car markets is likely, which will compromise the profitability of U.S. production and delay planned expansion. Assuming not all foreign producers remain in the U.S. market and that only a few add new assembly modules, production may reach 1.8 million annually by 2005.

Because these facilities use imported engines, transmissions and other parts, they create less domestic employment in the auto parts industry than the U.S. plants they displace. Some suppliers have located near the new plants, and more may relocate as the viability of the plants is proven, but the overall job creation potential of foreign assembly facilities is likely to be only about half that of a U.S. plant.

In addition, fewer of these facilities are likely to be in Michigan, compared to the state's current predominance as an auto producer. Of the seven foreign producers, only two have headquarters in the state, and only one will have production facilities there.

5. *The Development of the Upscale Market*

Continued growth of personal income, a proliferation of new models, and improvements in the technology and amenities of automobiles are likely to shift the automobile market upscale substantially over the next two decades. The aging of the baby boom into its most affluent years is likely to accelerate the trend. Throughout the postwar era, the average new automobile has been increasingly likely to be equipped with a wide range of options, ranging from stereos and air conditioners to pin stripes and velour seats. With some regularity, one year's fad becomes next year's standard equipment. The current popularity of high quality sound systems and digital displays suggests that the progression will continue. Based on one measure--the relationship between the average price of a new car and the

A CLOSE LOOK AT THE AUTOMOBILE INDUSTRY

price of the cheapest model available--the pure transportation value of the average car is now only about 40 percent of the average sales price.

Because upscale models with many options may require as many as 50 percent more man-hours than the lowest priced stripped down models, this trend will have a favorable impact on automobile employment in the U.S. and Michigan.

Imports are initially expected to continue to capture the low end of the U.S. auto market first, and so the number of jobs on assembly lines producing traditional American-made cars will be somewhat greater (approximately 8-12 percent) than they would otherwise be.

6. Michigan's Automotive Future--A Projection

How do these various factors fit together, and what will they mean for automobile production and employment in Michigan? One projection of auto sales, employment, and productivity gains is shown on the accompanying Figure.

As the projections show, employment in Michigan declines by almost half over the next two decades, with most of the loss resulting from increased productivity and higher imports.

Although such long range projections obviously carry many uncertainties, it is important to note that many of the variables that affect future employment will interact in ways that counterbalance each other, tending to make the forecast more likely to be accurate.

For example, if productivity increases more slowly than projected, employment would not decline as rapidly, but American cost competitiveness would erode, increasing imports and lowering employment. Similarly, if new producers from Korea or elsewhere in the Pacific Basin increased sales in the U.S., these new entrants would likely capture part of their share from what would otherwise have been Japanese import sales, leaving American production less affected. Tighter restraints might cut imports, but foreign manufacturers would probably respond by increasing production at domestic plants using imported parts.

In sum, no strategy or set of events is likely to prevent Michigan's automobile employment from declining. Though lower productivity growth or import restraints could slow the slide (just as recessions, slow economic growth, or rapid productivity growth could accelerate it), Michigan inevitably faces a future with many fewer jobs in automobile manufacturing.

A CLOSE LOOK AT THE AUTOMOBILE INDUSTRY

Figure 3-2

PROJECTIONS OF U.S. MOTOR VEHICLE PRODUCTION AND EMPLOYMENT TO 2005

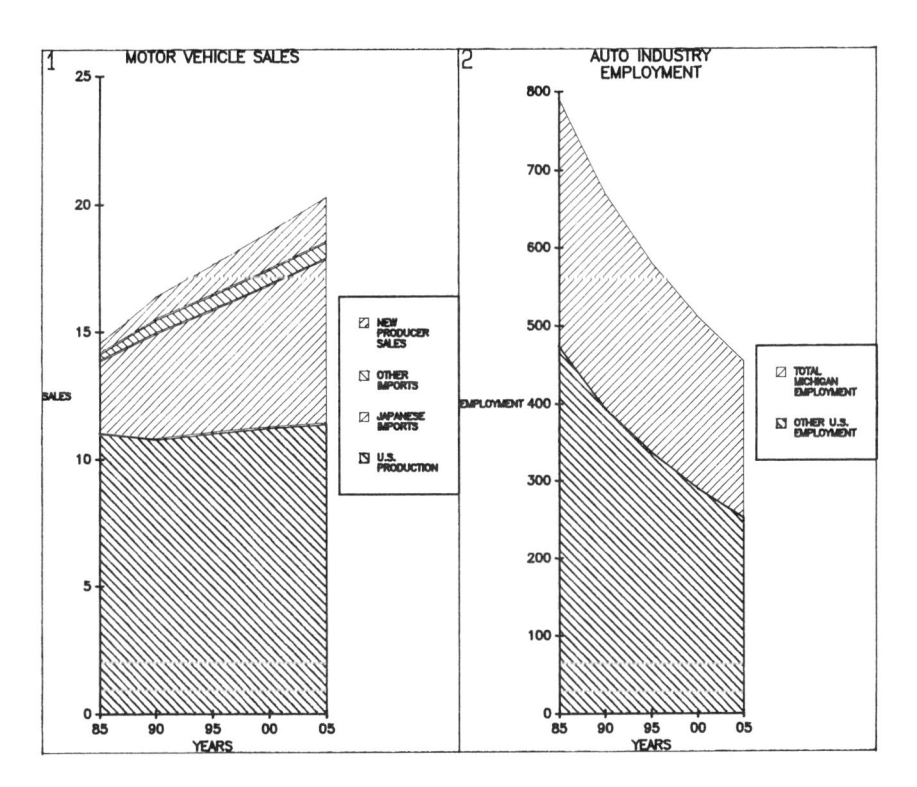

Source: Hudson Institute Projections.

Chapter 4
THE DEMOGRAPHIC TRENDS

A. A Changing Population

By national and Midwestern standards, Michigan is a relatively youthful state, but continuous out-migration has begun to alter its population composition. First, Michigan has not shared much in the recent national rise in births because the young adults it has lost are bearing their children elsewhere.[1] Whereas the state's percentage of population under age five was 3 percent above the national share in 1980, by mid-1984 it was 3 percent below the national share.

Second, although state data are lacking, migration seems to be changing the composition of regional households. In the early 1980s, 43 Michigan counties had migration deficits of 2 percent or more of population. Collectively, these counties lost 313,400 people (190,000 if Wayne County is excluded). Young people moving from the North helped to make married couples the fastest growing type of household in the West and South in 1980-84, whereas the North had an absolute decline in husband-wife families. Obviously, this change could augur even wider regional differences in births in the future--an important consideration when the next congressional reapportionment comes due.

Third, out-migration is making Michigan's population more parochial. Although the Detroit area's Arab population is the country's largest, Michigan was largely bypassed by the 1970s' influx of Hispanics and Asians. While the nation's foreign-born

---

[1]This seems to be true for blacks as well as whites: the black share of births in 34 southern Michigan counties fell from 21 percent in 1973 to about 19 percent in the late 1970s and early 1980s.

population was rising, Michigan's was falling 4.5 percent, of whom two-thirds are Europeans and Canadians (with a very high median age). Also contrary to the national trend, the proportion of Michigan residents born in-state rose to 72 percent. Because urban areas are a traditional haven for newcomers, it is notable that only two of Michigan's metro areas (Detroit and Ann Arbor) have a higher foreign-born share of population than the state as a whole, and only two (Benton Harbor and Ann Arbor) have a below-average proportion of Michigan-born residents. This proportion was 90 percent in the Bay City area and exceeded 80 percent in Grand Rapids, Saginaw, and Muskegon.

Internal Migration. Michigan's internal migration trends have resembled those of the nation at large. Growth in the 1970s was associated with college towns, state capitals, and "amenity-rich" rural areas. The Ann Arbor, Lansing, and Kalamazoo metro areas reflected a post-industrial development pattern combining relatively high population mobility, education, and women's employment with relatively low fertility and fewer manufacturing jobs. Northern Michigan achieved national note as eleven contiguous counties in the northern lower peninsula experienced an 84 percent population increase (compared to 4 percent for the state as a whole). The North's lure--other than tranquil surroundings and recreation--was often a low cost of living, which was attractive to retirees, to some low-wage employers, and to some of the unemployed.

But the North's gains in people and jobs were big only in percentage terms: the northern lower peninsula enjoyed a 23 percent jump in employment in 1972-83, but its share of the state's jobs rose only .7 percent. Populous southwestern Michigan's 16 percent gain in employment in this period ismore impressive. The Southwest also saw its share of Michigan's shrinking manufacturing jobs rise from 21 to 25 percent, despite serious weakness in the area nearest South Bend and Chicago.

Pronounced internal population shifts are old news for Michigan. Between 1910 and 1930, a solid majority of the state's counties suffered population shrinkage as opportunities to earn a decent living shifted from lumbering, mining, and farming

THE DEMOGRAPHIC TRENDS

to the auto industry and its suppliers. But in that period Wayne County grew by 255 percent (1.4 million), and such counties as Oakland and Genesee also contributed to Michigan's overall 70 percent growth. Both the gains and the losses from that era's industrial adjustments were dramatically evident within the state.

Urban Patterns. Until recently, the same could be said for the ever-volatile processes of urban evolution. Table 4-1, showing Michigan's 20 largest cities in 1960 and 1980, illustrates this volatility:

- o   Six cities, including the two northernmost, dropped off the top twenty between 1960 and 1980.
- o   Of their replacements, four cities were not even incorporated in 1960 (and 21st-ranked Farmington Hills was the largest new city incorporated in the entire United States in the 1970s).
- o   Detroit's share of the top twenty's population plummeted from 51 percent to 39 percent in 20 years.
- o   Detroit's suburbs loom large on both lists (but also among the dropouts).
- o   The population of 1980s top twenty was 12 percent smaller than the population of 1960s (although Michigan's total population was up by 18 percent).
- o   However, if the three biggest cities are excluded, the rest of the top twenty experienced a 25 percent rise in population.

These seemingly chaotic findings strongly reflect national trends: the declining density of large cities, the differentiation of older and newer suburbs, and (as noted earlier) the renewed vitality of many non-metropolitan areas. The difference from the past is that Michigan's share of the losses has come to outweigh its share of the gains, not merely during recessions but on a continuing basis. Because this condition is likely to persist even if the state's economy does well, the population changes it implies provide important clues to the future.

Table 4-1
MICHIGAN'S TWENTY LARGEST CITIES, 1960 AND 1980

1960			1980	
1. Detroit	1670.1		1. Detroit	1203.3
2. Flint	196.9		2. Grand Rapids	181.8
3. Grand Rapids	177.3		3. Warren	161.1
4. Dearborn	112.0		4. Flint	159.6
5. Lansing	107.8		5. Lansing	130.4
6. Saginaw	98.3		6. Sterling Heights	109.0
7. Warren	89.2		7. Ann Arbor	108.0
8. Pontiac	82.2		8. Livonia	104.8
9. Kalamazoo	82.1		9. Dearborn	90.7
10. Royal Oak	80.6		10. Westland	84.6
11. St. Clair Shores	76.7		11. Kalamazoo	79.7
12. Ann Arbor	67.3		12. Taylor	77.6
13. Livonia	66.7		13. Saginaw	77.5
14. Lincoln Park	53.9		14. Pontiac	76.3
15. Bay City	53.6		15. St. Clair Shores	76.2
16. Jackson	50.7		16. Southfield	75.6
17. Roseville	50.2		17. Royal Oak	70.9
18. Muskegon	46.5		18. Dearborn Heights	67.7
19. Wyoming	45.8		19. Troy	67.1
20. East Detroit	45.8		20. Wyoming	59.6
Total Population	3253.7			3061.9
Detroit's Share	51 %			39 %

Source: U.S. Bureau of the Census.

THE DEMOGRAPHIC TRENDS

B. The Aging Baby Boom

By 2005, the oversized generation born immediately after World War II will be nearing retirement and the prime age work force will be starting to shrink. For the next two decades, however, the demographic outlook is strikingly favorable:
The growth rate of the retirement-age population will be by far the slowest for any 20-year period in this century, with scarcely any decline in the ratio of working-age to pension-age Americans. Michigan's projected 1980-2000 increase at ages 65 and older is 212,000 (+23 percent), compared to 274,000 (+43 percent) in 1960-80 and 307,000 (+93 percent) in 1940-60. This moderation comes from the aging of the small cohorts born in the late 1920s and 1930s.
The stress of absorbing the baby-boom generation into the work force is ending. Peak to trough, the nation can expect a 21 percent drop in the numbers at labor force entry age in the 1980s and early 1990s. In manufacturing, this will ease adjustment to automation and related trends, and encourage new investments in labor-saving technology. In services, large numbers of low-skilled "kid jobs" will be replaced by smaller numbers of higher-skilled, higher-paying jobs through reorganization and more investment in technology. Redesign of jobs will also aim to increase employment of the elderly and handicapped.
The experience of youth scarcity will reinforce current concern about 20 years of national slippage in the schools: dwindling proficiency in basic skills, neglect of the "hard subjects" that are needed for competitiveness in the world economy, and laxity with respect to classroom behavior, truancy, and work habits. The prevailing perception will be: if we won't have quantity, we must have quality.
The number of workers will decline, not only at the inexperienced youngest ages, but also at the immediate pre-retirement ages, where productivity is sometimes depressed by health problems, outmoded skills, seniority protection, and a "serving-time" psychology. There will be fewer 55-to-64 year olds in 2000 than today. The key development in the work force will be the maturation of the biggest postwar cohorts from

their twenties to their forties. A rising proportion of the work force will combine health and vitality with solid experience and the seriousness that comes from family responsibilities (and heavy mortgages).

Federal population projections[2] assume that age-specific inter-state migration rates will be the same in the 1980s and 1990s as in the 1970s. These rates would give Michigan one percent population growth in the 1980s and a two percent decline in the 1990s, owing to dwindling numbers of women at child-bearing age.[3] This decline, projected for the North as a whole, would continue in the absence of positive changes in migration and/or fertility. So long as these changes do not occur, Michigan (and the North) will have less growth of growing age groups and more decline of dwindling ones than the nation as a whole.

Under this projection, Michigan's baby-boom generation shrinks from 3.5 million at ages 5-to-24 in 1970 to 2.8 million at ages 35-to-54 in 2000. However, as Table 4-2 and Figure 4-1 show, the size of this generation is still sufficient to produce much more growth during 1980-2000, at the basic homeowning, childraising ages of 30-to-49, than at any other lifestage: e.g., 31 percent vs. 23 percent for the elderly. In Michigan as nationally, depiction of the population as "aging" in this period is technically correct but seriously misleading.

---

[2]U.S. Bureau of the Census, "Provisional Projections of the Population of States, by Age and Sex: 1980-2000," *Current Population Reports*, Series P-25, No. 937, p. 24. These projections are based on the 1980 census. See also: Michigan Department of Management and Budget, "Population Projections for Michigan to the Year 2010," 1985.

[3]Federal population growth estimates are used in this report. Projections recently issued by Michigan show continued growth because out-migration is assumed to fall well below the 1970s rate. See Table 4-5, p. 79 for comparison to the federal projections.

THE DEMOGRAPHIC TRENDS

Table 4-2

MICHIGAN: PROJECTED CHANGES IN AGE-GROUP NUMBERS, 1980-2000

	1980-90	% Change 1990-2000	1980-2000
I. Lifestage			
Preschool Age (0-4)	+7%	-17%	-11%
School Age (5-14)	-11	-1	-12
Young Adult (15-29)	-15	-16	-29
Nesting Age (30-49)	+27	+3	+31
Empty Nest Age (50-64)	-10	+16	+4
Elderly (65+)	+20	+3	+23
Total Pop.	+1	-2	-.5
II. 5-Year Age Groups			
0-4	+7%	-17%	-11%
5-9	-3	-7	-10
10-14	-18	+5	-13
15-19	-25	-3	-27
20-24	-20	-19	-35
25-29	+2	-25	-24
30-34	+17	-20	-6
35-39	+33	0	+33
40-44	+44	+14	+64
45-49	+19	+30	+54
50-54	-12	+41	+24
55-59	-18	+19	+2
60-64	0	-12	-12
65-69	+10	-18	-10
70-74	+16	-1	+15
75-79	+24	+11	+37
80-84	+29	+20	+54
85+	+48	+40	+107

Source: U.S. Census Bureau, "Provisional Projections of the Population of States, by Age and Sex: 1980-2000," Current Population Reports, Series P-25, No. 937; P.24.

Figure 4-1

MICHIGAN 1980-2000: THE BABY BOOM AGES POPULATION SHARE

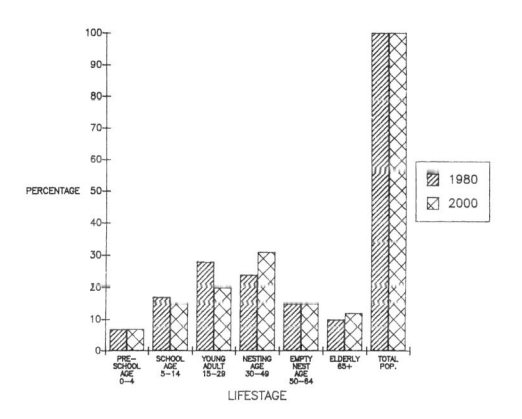

C. The Drought of Young Workers

In addition to growth of middle-aged groups, the demographic outlook also suggests a decline at labor force entry ages that is especially sharp in the 1985-95 decade. Michigan's net decline at ages 15-to-29 between 1980 and 2000 is projected at more than twice the national figure. This is the aftermath of enormous regional differences in the national "baby bust": between 1961 and 1978, the number of children under five fell by 36 percent in the Northwest, 32 percent in the Midwest, 18 percent in the South, and 8 percent in the West. As these children come of age, the rapidity of the shrinkage could have major consequences for Michigan.

Apart from the potential benefits from easing of youth unemployment, the numeric and compositional outlook for young workers suggests the possibility of critical scarcities in more demanding occupational specialties. Filling new jobs and replacing younger technical and managerial personnel who may choose to leave the state will become much more difficult in the next ten years than in the past. Qualitative improvements in Michigan's schools are not merely important but urgent. Demographic conditions of the next ten years will make employers' locational decisions exceptionally sensitive to workers' locational preferences. The state's policies to promote economic development should focus on attracting and retaining young workers as well as employers. Unless this is done effectively, the projected stabilization of the numbers of young workers toward the century's end will not last to 2005.

D. The Aging of Suburbia

Although the retiree population will be increasing at a slower rate in the next 20 years, an accelerated aging trend will occur in many suburbs near Detroit. These communities, whose growth exploded during the catch-up construction after World War II, will increasingly consist of older housing and aging families. In the 1970s, the "graying" of such suburbs meant a

THE DEMOGRAPHIC TRENDS

shift of their age bulge of early settlers from ages 40-to-54 to ages 50-to-64. For example, while 50-to-64s' share of the total population fell from 17 to 15 percent in Detroit and rose from 14 to 15 percent in Michigan as a whole, it jumped from 11 to 18 percent in Warren and from 10 to 19 percent in Livonia (see Table 4-3).

Although the elderly proportion of the population doubled in many such suburbs, it usually remained well below the state's average. This will change as the 1980s 50-to-64 year olds become the 1990s 60-to-74s and the 2000s 70-to-84s. It will change even if retirement migration out of such areas is high. The negative effects of the age-bulge will initially be felt as a slight depression of local commerce, as pre-retirement incomes fall to post-retirement levels, and perhaps in more resistance to school taxes (by people with plenty of time to lobby for their political interests). Over time, more of the postwar suburbs' retirement bulge will become frail or handicapped. At that stage, demands on local government will grow and standards of home maintenance will decline.

Less visibly, the occupation of a rising fraction of postwar suburbs' housing by retired people means that this housing is not available for families with children. Already in the 1970s, the maturing of the dominant age group from "nesting age" to "empty nest age" gave some suburbs in the Detroit area 40-55 percent declines in numbers of children under five, compared to 29 percent for Detroit City, 15 percent for the state, and 5 percent for the United States. In some suburbs, the demographic changes illustrated in Table 4-3 have undercut support for the schools, reducing their attractiveness to families with children.

One aspect of this "aging suburb" phenomenon pertains to employers who rely heavily on postwar suburbs (and similar areas within central cities) to house their workers. In Detroit, for example, it is likely that more employers will vacate the core in the next ten-to-twenty years, specifically because too few attractive neighborhoods for family-raising exist within reasonable commuting range of their facilities.

MICHIGAN BEYOND 2000

Table 4-3

DETROIT'S GRAYING SUBURBS: SELECTED AGE GROUPS' SHARE OF POPULATION, AND PERCENT CHANGE IN NUMBERS, 1970-80

	Warren 1970	1980	% Change	Livonia 1970	1980	% Change
Total Pop.	172,260	161,134	-10%	110,109	103,814	- 5%
Ages Under 5	10%	5%	-53	9%	6%	-41
50-64	11	18	+45	10	19	+75
65+	4	8	+86	4	8	+67

	Saint Clair Shores 1970	1980	% Change	Southgate 1970	1980	% Change
Total Pop.	88,093	76,210	-13%	33,909	32,058	- 5
Ages Under 5	8%	5%	-49	9%	6%	- 37
50-64	13	22	+44	11	19	+ 63
65+	6	11	+65	3	7	+121

	Wayne County, Excluding Detroit 1970	1980	% Change	State of Michigan 1970	1980	% Change
Total Pop.	1,155,269	1,134,552	- 2%	8,875,000	9,262,000	+ 4%
Ages Under 5	9%	7%	-24	9%	7%	-15
2 50-64	14	17	+22	14	15	+10
65+	7	9	+35	9	10	+21

	Detroit 1970	1980	% Change
Total Pop.	1,511,482	1,203,339	20%
Ages Under 5	9%	8%	-29
50-64	17	15	-27
65+	12	12	-19

Source: U.S. Census, 1980, Vol. PC80-1-B24 Mich., Tables 19, 26, 33, 46.

THE DEMOGRAPHIC TRENDS

E. Migration in Michigan: Outstate and Out of the State

If nothing changes but demography, Michigan will have a lower out-migration rate in the 1990s than in the 1980s. As the number of Michigan residents in the 18 to 24 age group declines in the years to come, the large number of long-distance moves associated with college, military service, first job, and "just trucking" will dwindle. Other things being equal, Michigan residents will be significantly less mobile ten years hence and a higher proportion of movers will be in their thirties and forties. The data will *look* like an improvement, even if nothing has changed but age composition. It is important not to be misled.

Depending on job availability and local cordiality to growth, the probable migration trends of the coming years will:

- o spur the northward sprawl of Michigan's urban south;
- o fuel new growth centers in northern Michigan;
- o favor the southwestern over the southeastern part of the state;
- o benefit southeastern exurbs over pricey suburbs; and/or
- o lose people Michigan most needs to keep.

Probably all of these things will happen to some degree, the issue being their proportional importance.

The reason that Michigan is still a relatively young state compared to the rest of the nation is that, over the 1945-75 period, the state did better at attracting migrants than other parts of the Midwest. These migrants came for *jobs*. Gallup surveys from the 1950s found Michigan ranking third (after New York and California) in perceived economic opportunities.

More recently, Michigan has lost its status as a beacon of opportunity. Weakening of Michigan's migration magnet helps to explain why gaining areas within the state have recently been counties with a high proportion of older people. Northern counties that have for generations been sending their young people south are now seeing them return upon retirement.

Population Redistribution. The prospect for substantial reductions in automotive employment and the potential for large early retirement programs could significantly boost intrastate migration to the northern and western parts of the state. The only up-to-date statistical forecast of Michigan's internal population changes are the state-developed population projections. While these numbers may be overly optimistic in their totals, the *relative* growth displayed for counties in these projections is worth attention. When the projections are aggregated to divide the lower peninsula into northern, central, and southern regions, the southern region's population share slips only marginally in 1985-2005--from 80.6 percent to 79.4 percent--and the upper peninsula's share from 3.5 percent to 3.4 percent. The biggest share gainer, the northern lower peninsula, goes only from 4.4 percent to 5.4 percent of the state's population. In this tripartite division of the lower peninsula, the north grows fastest (+32.5 percent), the center is middling (+10.7 percent), and the south grows slowest (+6.7 percent) (see Table 4-4).

However, southern Michigan's lion's share of the state's population calls for further division. When this is done laterally, the double tier of counties extending from St. Clair and Macomb to Ottawa and Allegan shows higher 20-year growth than the peninsula's central latitudes, while "southern southern" Michigan--from Wayne and Monroe to Van Buren and Berrien counties--has a slight population decline. When an east-west division is added, all latitudes of the lower peninsula show more vigor in their western than in their eastern half.

In effect, these projections say that the tendency of the urban south to sprawl northward more than southward will persist. The north-moving boundary of the urban south (suburbs and exurbs) will continue to be a stronger growth force than autonomous development in the peninsula's central latitudes

THE DEMOGRAPHIC TRENDS

Table 4-4

STATE-PROJECTED DISTRIBUTIONAL OUTLOOK FOR MICHIGAN'S POPULATION, 1985-2005

Regional Shares	1985	2005
Upper Peninsula	3.5%	3.4%
Lower Peninsula		
Northern	4.4	5.4
Central	11.6	11.8
Southern	80.6	79.4

% Change	1985 - 2005	
Upper Peninsula	+ 4.7%	
Lower Peninsula		
Northern	+32.5	
Central	+10.7	
Southern	+ 6.7	
--Northern Part	+13.4	
--Southern Part	- .2	
	Eastern	Western
Lower Peninsula		
Northern	+27.1%	+37.2%
Central	+ 9.5	+13.2
Southern	+ 4.7	+13.8
--Northern Part	+11.1	+20.8
--Southern Part	- 1.6	+ 5.3

Source: Michigan Department of Management and Budget, *Population Projections for Michigan to the Year 2010, Summary Report*, Lansing, March 1985.

where ailing urban centers (Bay City, Saginaw, Muskegon) counterbalance the growth of small places.

The west-favoring pattern of growth does not lend itself to generalization. In the northern part of the lower peninsula, the Traverse Bay area is becoming a significant population center, while the northeast has no major growth centers and a long-stagnant economy bludgeoned by plant closings. In central as in southern Michigan, the eastern half is the more affluent, but will not grow as rapidly because of dwindling labor demand in the auto industry. Although the westernmost metro areas (Muskegeon, Benton Harbor) are troubled, the southwest as a whole has population-growth advantages associated with more balanced metro economies, and perhaps also with smaller metro scale and lesser urban problems.

The relative trends shown in the state's projections seem most likely to err in understating the growth disadvantages of the southeast and central-east metro areas. However, good highway access to many undeveloped parts of central and northern Michigan creates the potential for compensatory non-metro gains, based on manufacturing and perhaps also on the types of office industry rendered footloose by modern telecommunications.

THE DEMOGRAPHIC TRENDS

Table 4-5

AGE GROUP PROJECTIONS FOR MICHIGAN: THE STATE'S PROJECTIONS AS A RATIO TO THE FEDERAL PROJECTIONS FOR THE STATE, 1990 AND 2000

Ages	1990	2000
0-4	.90	1.18
5-9	.96	1.12
10-14	1.02	1.04
15-19	1.05	1.03
20-24	1.06	1.13
25-29	.97	1.11
30-34	1.00	1.11
35-39	1.01	1.03
40-44	.99	1.05
45-49	.98	1.06
50-54	.98	1.03
55-59	1.00	1.03
60-64	1.05	1.06
65-69	1.07	1.10
70-74	1.04	1.12
75+	.84	.81

Comments: Federal projections yield a Michigan population of 9.4 million in 1990 and 9.2 million in 2000. These projections assume the persistence of 1970s' interstate migration rates. The state's own populations take early 1980s' losses into account but assume a more favorable balance later in the 1980-2010 period. Under the state's assumptions, Michigan's population grows to 9.4 million in 1990, 9.8 million in 2000, and 10.0 million in 2010. (The federal projection, carried forward, would show further population decline in 2010.)

For 1990, the state's projections are more than 2 percent in excess of the federal projections at ages 15-24 and 60-74. But the state's projections for 2000 are more than 2 percent above the federal projections at all ages but 75 and older, for which the federal figures are much higher for both 1990 and 2000. The state's projections for 2000 exceed the federal projections by 10 percent or more at ages 0-9, 20-34, and 65-74. This indicates a very favorable migration assumption for persons who retire, and for young adults and their children.

Sources: U.S. Bureau of the Census; Michigan Department of Management and Budget.

Chapter 5

SOCIAL AND POLITICAL TRENDS

A. The Changing Role of Government

One of the fundamental trends of the industrial revolution has been the increase in the share of income going to government. In .part this reflects the increasing regulatory role of government necessitated by the greater complexity and interdependence of society. In part it reflects a series of collective decisions in most developed countries to use government as the instrument for delivering many services to all citizens and for improving the conditions of life for the poor and disadvantaged.

The result is that both the regulatory and the financial roles of government have grown relentlessly throughout much of this century.

Against this background, the current trends in federal, state, and local government policies appear to be on sharply different courses. Federal spending and regulation for social purposes have ceased their growth. The state and local roles, on the other hand, show no signs of similar retrenchment, and indeed may be expanding to assume greater responsibility.

Since 1900, the United States has experienced three dramatic waves of innovative federal social legislation: the 1920s, the 1950s, and the present. This recurrent federal activism was made possible by a revolution in transport and communications technology that shaped a mosaic of local cultures into an American culture.

One key issue for the future is whether the centralizing trend of social legislation and its funding will persist, perhaps with a new creative surge in the 1990s. Precedent favors this projection, but present evidence supports a conjecture that the focus of innovation and responsibility will continue shifting back to the states. Hindsight mar regard centralization as an *industrial-era* trend, and deconcentration ("small is beautiful") as the true post-industrial thrust, with a new sorting out of federal-state roles.

A second key issue stemming from the technology-based emergence of a national culture is the increased volatility of social policy. Modern communications have accelerated the rate at which attitudes and opinions spread across the country. This places unrelenting and ever-changing pressures on government to act in haste. It helps to explain why the major federal legislative initiatives of the mid-1960s are so much less securely institutionalized twenty years later than were the regulatory innovations of the Progressive Era and such landmarks of the New Deal as Social Security pensions, public assistance, and the minimum wage. For Michigan, the potential for vast swings in public policy poses particular hazards. With the state narrowly balanced in political terms, and subject to wide fluctuations in economic conditions, shifting public pressures could cause state policies to fluctuate unpredictably over the next two decades. The recent history of the income tax surcharge could be only the first of a series of such episodes.

1. The Loss of Federal Aid

Twenty years ago, the federal "war on poverty" allocated $11 million to Michigan, half to Detroit. Detroit's Common Council was not elated. Its federal aid hopes focused on a $250 million plan for "the finest cultural center in the world." The Council's majority felt that the purposes of the new Community Action Program were already being met adequately by other means.

Times changed. Only one building of the cultural center materialized (without federal aid), but Washington's financial coverage of Detroit's operating expenses leaped to 24-27 percent in 1976-81. Michigan's vigorous participation in poverty and urban programs yielded a 1250 percent increase in its annual federal aid between 1962 and 1982 (from $290 million to $4 billion). From 1969 to 1980, the state's rank in federal aid per capita improved from 44th to 20th. This occurred in context with enormous national increases: by 1976, federal aid to states and localities was equivalent to 34 percent of their revenues from their own sources.

But this figure dropped to 24 percent in 1984 and is projected at 22 percent in FY 1986. The federal share of Detroit's operating revenues is down to 13 percent and will fall more with the scheduled termination of revenue-sharing. Will the new trend last 20 years? This is actually two questions for Michigan.

The first pertains to diminished political support for the federal poverty programs that have given Michigan more than its proportional share of federal aid: in FY 1984, Michigan's chunk of the federal-aid pie was slightly above its 3.7 percent share of the U.S. population, but the state drew 7.8 percent of all federal spending for welfare, 4.4 percent for Medicaid, 5.5 percent for low-income home energy assistance, and 7.2 percent for UDAG grants.

The current trend away from increases in public spending for aid to the poor may not persist over 20 years. However, federal programs of these kinds that shift money to northern states and older cities have a weakening political constituency. In 1982, the South and West for the first time gained a majority in the Congress; the U.S. center of population has now moved west of the Mississippi. No matter how adroitly Michigan's members of Congress work to shape new coalitions, the state and its cities will have less political muscle than in the past.

The second question is whether total federal aid to state and local governments will resume its rise sufficiently for Michigan to benefit even with a dwindling national share. The outlook is definitely weak for the next ten years and perhaps for much longer. The magnitude of projected federal deficits is a persuasive reason for this expectation, but a more important factor in the long run is the long-term decline of differences among states in ability to support governmental programs from their own resources. For example, Michigan's advantage over Georgia in per capita personal income diminished from 86 percent in 1943 to 36 percent in 1963 and 10 percent in 1983.

MICHIGAN BEYOND 2000

The powerful trend of inter-state income convergence increasingly raises questions as to whether geographically redistributive federal programs convey enough national benefit to justify the transaction costs of funneling the money through Washington. Considering also that a greatly increased proportion of federal aid is disbursed through formula grants that do little to endear Congressmen to the folks back home, the reduced economic rationale for many forms of federal aid will increase the political appeal of responding to deficit pressures by "dumping" more social funding responsibilities on the states.

The ability to raise taxes to support new spending may also be shifting from the federal government to the states. A 1984 survey by the Advisory Commission on Intergovernmental Relations (ACIR) found that the federal government has moved from top to bottom in the public's view of return on their tax dollars. Other surveys find the average American believing that 29-43 percent of every federal tax dollar is "wasted."

In sum, the only responsible planning assumption for Michigan's state government in 1985 is that the new era in federal-state relations will show considerable staying power. At the present point, early in this era, Michigan derives 26 percent of its state-government revenue from Washington. Much goes to the poor: e.g., 60 percent to social and medical services, compared to 26 percent of the state's revenues from its own sources. But a federal-aid dollar is also four times as likely as a Michigan dollar to be spent on economic development efforts.

It is worthwhile to list a small sample of state agencies' concerns with recently proposed funding cuts, as an indicator of the range of potential impacts:

o   An end to Urban Development Action Grants that are said to have leveraged a billion dollars in private investment in Detroit and other Michigan cities;
o   A jump in the average price of school lunches per paying child from 95 to $1.30 or more;

SOCIAL AND POLITICAL TRENDS

o   Elimination of the state's private forest development program;
o   Doubling of the state's spending burden for the Superfund hazardous waste program;
o   Loss by Medicaid of 75 percent in matching funds for information processing and 90 percent for management systems development (plus the hazard of a cap on federal Medicaid and ADC money);
o   Reductions in the state's share of $4.7 billion in federal highway funds, plus withdrawal of Amtrak, local mass transit, and airport subsidies.

Spending Priorities. Either shrinkage or changing priorities for the federal share of Michigan's public spending constitutes an important *de facto* change in the state's own policies. With both of these developments likely to occur on a significant scale, reliance on piecemeal *ad hoc* responses can cumulatively inflate state spending and skew its distribution among functions in ways that lack rational justification or majority support.

This hazard arises on top of the usual menu of legislative choices: the Legislature and Governor annually see dozens of specialized studies that aim to guide state policy, often urging new initiatives in such areas (to cite current examples) as hospital rate regulation, preventive health care, and the management of toxic waste disposal. In the new reduced federal-aid era, the choices forced by Congressional action will make it all the more important to set priorities carefully when considering new spending initiatives.

In the long run, reduced federal aid may be beneficial to Michigan. The lavish inflow has been a mixed blessing. It has certainly skewed many of Michigan's spending priorities from projects that were high on the state's list of needs to ones that fit the narrow definition of categorical aid programs. And it has often saddled the state with high operating costs and burdensome or coercive regulations.

However, the steps Michigan must take to gain better control of its governmental future are likely to be difficult. Because federal aid cost control is driven by budgetary politics, the forms it takes may bear little resemblance to a rational redistribution of governmental functions between federal and state levels. Further, a rational transition would entail federal tax cuts. The real transition will involve tax increases and/or loss of deductibility of state-local taxes. For Michigan--a state with relatively high taxes, a highly cyclical economy, and a major industrial restructuring--this outlook suggests special difficulty in balancing the needs of the disadvantaged with the demands of vested interests and the requirements for economic competitiveness.

Finally, federal aid is only part of the federal money flow that balances Michigan's federal taxes. Michigan ranks near the bottom in total inflow per dollar of federal taxes, in per capita inflow for all defense functions, and in domestic procurement inflow. The procurement rankings have a different connotation from recent slippage in federal aid rank. Michigan's budget director blurred this distinction when he wrote that "the emphasis of the Reagan Administration on shifting more dollars into defense at the expense of domestic programs only exacerbates the inequity." No issue of equity is involved; rather it may be that Michigan's willingness to compete for federal business has not matched its willingness to compete for federal aid.

2. The Growing Role of States and Localities

The slower growth of federal domestic spending has not been matched by a parallel shrinkage in public demands for services. If these demands keep growing, a smaller federal role will lead to greater state and local responsibilities. In the short term, this is almost certain to happen, as federal dollars lost are replaced with state and local spending.

Table 5-1 presents the twenty-year trends in state and local spending. The table shows an index of spending per thousand dollars of personal income (the Spending Index, or SI) eliminating the effects of inflation and the growing economy from the picture.

SOCIAL AND POLITICAL TRENDS

Table 5-1

33 LARGEST STATES: TOTAL STATE-LOCAL GOVERNMENT SPENDING PER $1000 OF PERSONAL INCOME AND SPENDING ON EDUCATION AND WELFARE, RANKING IN 1962 AND 1982

TOTAL 1962		TOTAL 1982		EDUCATION 1962		EDUCATION 1982		WELFARE 1962		WELFARE 1982	
LA	$200	NY	$230	AZ	$73	OR	$83	KY	$31	NY	$40
MISS	198	OR	219	MISS	70	SC	80	OK	31	CA	35
KY	170	MINN	215	TX	68	AZ	79	MISS	21	MASS	34
AZ	167	MISS	214	MINN	65	MISS	77	COL	20	MINN	33
MINN	162	LA	210	OR	65	WIS	76	ALA	19	*MICH*	31
ORE	161	WIS	203	COL	64	ALA	74	ARK	18	PA	28
OK	157	*MICH*	193	LA	64	MINN	74	KY	15	WIS	26
WASH	157	ALA	192	WASH	64	*MICH*	73	MINN	15	ILL	24
ALA	154	AZ	190	IOWA	60	NC	73	GEO	14	KY	24
TEX	152	CAL	189	KAN	60	IOWA	72	MASS	14	MISS	24
WIS	152	GEO	185	CAL	59	LA	72	MO	14	OHIO	24
CAL	151	SC	184	IND	59	COL	71	WASH	14	OK	22
COL	151	WASH	182	*MICH*	58	WASH	70	CAL	13	IOWA	21
KAN	149	OK	180	OK	57	OK	69	IOWA	12	LA	21
ARK	148	IOWA	178	ALA	56	ARK	67	KAN	12	NJ	21
IOWA	146	MASS	178	KY	56	IND	67	OR	12	ARK	20
GEO	145	MD	177	ARK	54	NY	67	ILL	11	CONN	20
MICH	144	COL	176	SC	54	KAN	65	NY	11	GEO	19
TENN	143	KY	176	WIS	54	TEX	63	OHIO	11	SC	19
FLA	139	KAN	170	GEO	50	CAL	62	TENN	11	MD	18
NY	138	NC	170	NC	49	GEO	62	TX	11	ORE	18
SC	131	ARK	168	FLA	48	KY	62	WIS	11	TENN	18

87

SOCIAL AND POLITICAL TRENDS

As the table documents, Michigan's state and local spending has increased in parallel with the national average. From 1962 to 1982, Michigan's SI rose by about one third, from $144 per thousand dollars of personal income to $193. Compared to other Great Lakes states, Michigan occupied a middle position, below Minnesota and Wisconsin but above Ohio, Indiana, and Illinois (see Table 5-1).

But the impression of Michigan as "average" breaks down when spending components are separated (Figure 5-1). Relative to all state-local governments, Michigan experienced a much sharper decline in its SI for highway construction and maintenance (-52 percent vs. -36 percent) between 1957 and 1982, and a vastly greater increase in the index for welfare[1] (+315 percent vs. +141 percent; see Figure 5-2). Among the Great Lakes states, Michigan was spending less on welfare, in relation to income, in 1957 and 1962 than all but Indiana. By 1977 it was spending more than any Great Lakes state except Wisconsin, and in 1982 more than any but Minnesota. Moreover, all of the Great Lakes states--together with all the large northeastern states and California--experienced a much greater proportional increase in means-tested programs' share of state income than did the nation at large. Michigan was a leader in this surge.

Michigan's rise from below-average to far above average status in welfare spending demonstrates the general point: these states' SI for welfare rose initially because they were prosperous; they were acquiring a "post-industrial" willingness to spend more to aid the (then) dwindling minority of economically disadvantaged.

Federal and state spending for aid to the poor has recently declined for a variety of reasons: disillusionment with the "change agent" programs of the 1960s, loss of confidence in Washington's competence, economic difficulties in most of the

---

[1]"Welfare" includes all means-tested programs. Thus Medicaid is included under "welfare," not under "health and hospitals."

MICHIGAN BEYOND 2000

Figure 5-1

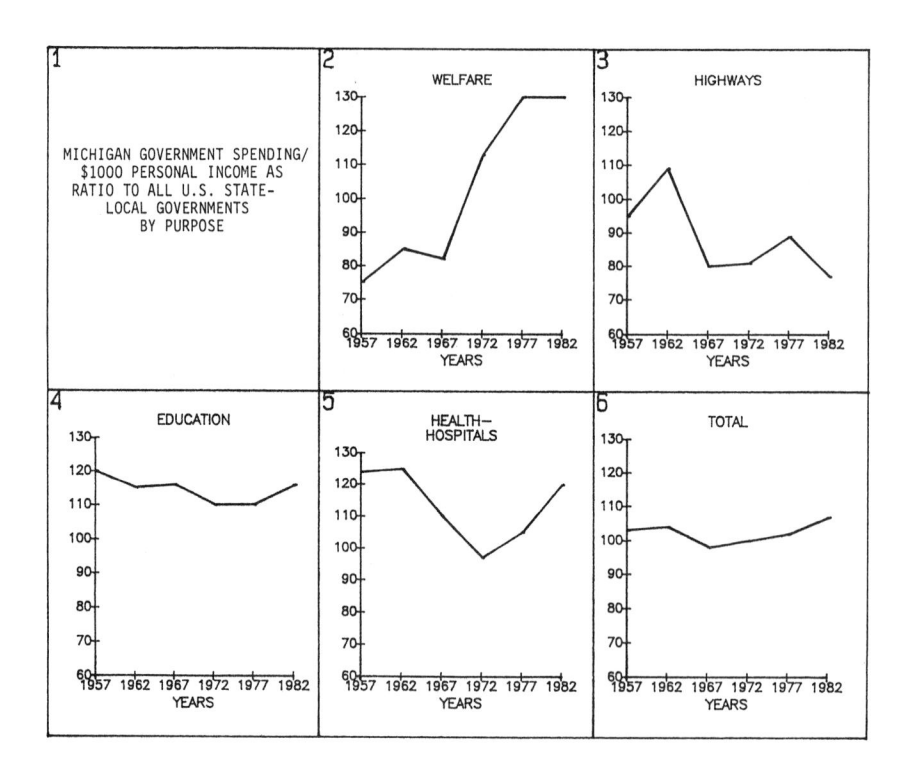

SOCIAL AND POLITICAL TRENDS

Figure 5-2

GREAT LAKE STATES AND U.S.: RATIOS TO MICHIGAN FOR TOTAL STATE AND LOCAL GOVERNMENT SPENDING PER $1000 PERSONAL INCOME IN CENSUS OF GOVERNMENT YEARS

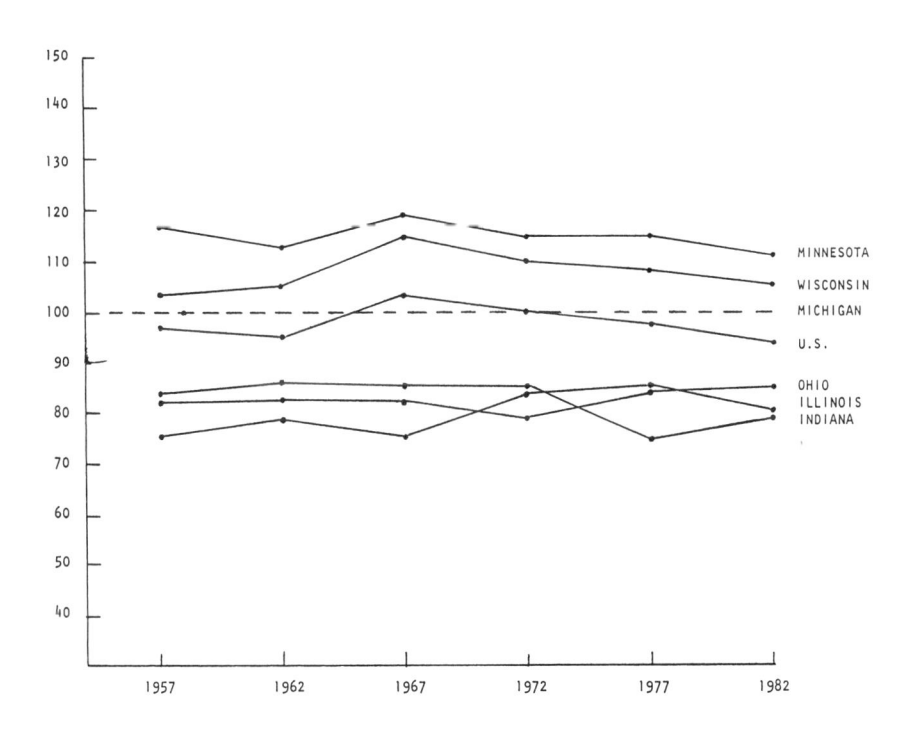

heavy spending states, and federal budget problems that point up the political weakness of the poor themselves. However in a 20-year outlook, the trend toward spending a rising share of income for the disadvantaged is likely to resume. For Example, today as in the early 1960s, Michigan and the nation are seeing a rising willingness to invest in education and training to improve the labor market value of low-income youth. Although there is little enthusiasm today for other social initiatives of the recent past--welfare as a right, outreach efforts to maximize program participation, income redistribution as "social justice"--such concepts may return to fashion if national economic growth is sustained.

At present, Michigan is subject to both forces that tend to raise the SI: (1) sluggish income growth--for the first time, the state's per capita income slipped below the national average in the early 1980s, and it remained there in 1984, and (2) psychologies of affluence that elevate public pressure for government spending. In the welfare area, two recent developments stand out. The first is that, despite economic recovery, Michigan's combined Aid to Dependent Children (ADC) and General Assistance (GA) caseload is one and a half times the size it was in 1979 (with the more-rapid GA increase uncushioned by federal aid). Second, despite economic uncertainty, the state recently chose to add adult dental coverage to its Medicaid program.

The first of these developments was primarily a response to greater needs, not merely at the worst of the recession (when 37 percent of Detroit's population qualified as "poor"), but averaged over the business cycle. But the second was basically an enforced act, in harmony with Michigan's political liberalism, and influenced by the prospect that the state's poor economic performance would result in Washington picking up a larger share of the ADC and Medicaid bill. In another state, this silver lining to a dark cloud might have been used to free-up state funds for other purposes. For example, resources might have been reallocated to highways, where Michigan has conspicuously lagged the nation's rate of public investment, or for education where, despite bipartisan agreement on the importance

SOCIAL AND POLITICAL TRENDS

of new spending, the state's performance is only moderately better than national norms. Or it might have been used for tax relief. In Michigan, there was no evaluation of state spending priorities. Instead a post-industrial attitude took precedence over strategic decisions on how to allocate limited resources.

B. Three Post-Industrial Issues: Education, Health Care and the Environment

1. Improving Education: Will Another Reform Succeed?

Despite long-standing bipartisan agreement on the importance of education, Michigan, like the rest of the nation, has been unable to find a formula that assures delivery of high quality, cost-effective education to the state's residents. In many ways, education is a relic of the past in terms of organization and the application of technology. The productivity of a classroom hour is not clearly greater today than it was a century ago.

In Michigan, the impact of the industrial era is reflected in an 88 percent reduction in the number of school districts over the past 30 years, and in modern equipment and teaching styles that seem necessary to hold the attention of children weaned on television (but have no documented influence on learning). These trends are typical of the nation at large. Michigan is different in its greater adherence to the tradition of local control, and in its exceptionally high teacher salaries: second to Alaska in a federal survey, and third to Alaska and New York in an NEA survey. This fits with the state's generally high wage pattern, and is balanced by 48th rank in the ratio of teachers to students.

Are Michigan's teachers unusually productive? The answer is probably not. Although Michigan's state administered achievement tests cannot be compared with national norms, its American College Testing scores for college admission are only slightly above average. The small proportion of its students that took Scholastic Aptitude Tests in 1982 ranked 24th in the nation, but a study that adjusted for students' socioeconomic status lowered this rank to a tie for 34th.

Many studies have shown that the socioeconomic background of students is much more important than funding levels in determining a school's rank in measured academic achievement. Other studies show that a principal's commitment to elevate measured achievement can work wonders in the "success" of schools with socioeconomically disadvantaged students. Both findings are predictable for a "pre-industrial" institution. Nationally, measured achievement soared after the "sputnik shock" of the late 1950s, and plummeted after the widespread acceptance of "post-industrial" values in the mid-1960s. Compared, for example, to the steady improvement in public health and longevity that followed increases in health care spending during the same period, the return on investment in education was disappointing.

The key message for Michigan is that the schools will go on trying, with some success, to follow the latest fashions in education. But these fashions are based on political judgments, not scientific evidence. The priorities pressed on teachers can affect what is taught and styles of teaching, but they do not seem to change educational productivity. For this reason, educational progress can be attenuated or sabotaged if too many interests jump on fashion's latest bandwagon. The pressure to add health and career education to Michigan's achievement tests is an example. These objectives are logically related to the renewed emphasis on teaching the skills to improve the quality of Michigan's work force and the competitiveness of its industries. However, when schools lack technical means to improve rates of learning, priorities for use of teaching time require harder-headed selectivity than political decisionmaking processes usually supply.

Demographic Influences. Michigan's schools today also suffer from two demographic stresses. First, the average Michigan school district (K to 12) may have no overall increase in school enrollment in this century, and the state will share in the continuing national trend of a rising proportion of youth coming from disadvantaged backgrounds. For high schools and colleges, most of the enrollment decline lies ahead, entailing hazards to curricular variety and teacher competence that were much less important for the elementary grades. Second, there has been an increase in the median age of teachers--from under-30 to 45. Older teachers, like older employees of all kinds, are harder to retrain and to motivate. They may be slow to adapt to new technologies or to new forms of organization. For the Michigan school system, the task ahead is analogous to that faced by the auto industry. It must retrain and motivate an aging work force to accomplish a more difficult task. It must promote universal competence in basic skills, increasing the pool of students who are able and motivated to go on to more demanding educational challenges. To succeed, it must adopt new technologies, learn new skills, and give up cherished institutional and organizational frameworks.

For example, the nine month school year that was structured in an agrarian era to enable children to help with work on the farm is clearly an anachronism in a highly technical society. Similarly, educational systems that specify how to teach and emphasize teachers' credentials, rather than measuring student performance and holding teachers accountable for that performance, have missed the basic lessons of management science proven over the last 50 years.

Most importantly, the Michigan schools might benefit from a much more aggressive deployment of technology, especially computers and telecommunications systems. Although there is continuing debate over the benefits and cost-effectiveness of computers and the like in the schools, they appear to hold the promise of finally breaking free of the tyranny of time constraints.

Students and teachers could have ready access to computers. They could "check them out," like library books. Instructors could utilize them to maintain detailed records of student's academic achievement, to identify students strengths and weaknesses, and to suggest individual learning plans. This strategy could help overcome a serious problem that teachers face today--how to teach a class of 25 individuals, each with his or her own best pace and style of learning.

Computers could also "teach" home-bound students via existing phone lines. Or, for that matter, cable television channels dedicated to broadcasting public school programs could be made interactive (i.e., two way video, one way video) and students who are too sick to go to school could still attend classes.

Computers could also take charge of drill and practice, lecturing, and testing; they could transform the role of the teacher. Rather than the delivery mechanism for information, the teacher could become more of a manager of instruction, a discussion leader, and a guide to students.

Such a change is tremendously threatening to many. Not only might teaching jobs be lost, but many traditional teachers might not be able to succeed in the new environment. For others, including both teachers and parents, computers and other technologies represent a depersonalization of education that is as objectionable as the assembly line was to earlier generations. This route to efficiency seems wholly at odds with what is observed of post-industrial value trends, helping to explain why its introduction lags enthusiasts' expectations.

It may be that, within 20 years, biogenetic research will transform the issue for education, making it possible to raise the learning potential of children before they reach the schools, and generating policy problems of cost, capability, and ethics such as are today familiar in medicine. But today's issues are more mundane:

- o First, what priorities should be established in a pre-industrial system where increasing instructional time seems to be the only way to teach more;
- o Second, what are the chances for industrial-type advance in productivity per class hour, and thereby in ability to serve more priorities at once? Can a rapidly aging work force be

SOCIAL AND POLITICAL TRENDS

managed and motivated to accept and implement such a change?

Michigan is on record as wanting to spend more for education--its Democratic governor and its Republican state school board concur on this point. It is not clear that more spending will work better, just as it is not clear that greater state control of how money is used would yield better "results." A more sophisticated grasp of the limits and possibilities of the educational system is the key to sound strategies.

2. Health Care: "Can Costs be Controlled?"

The great care with which the Social Security pension system was designed in 1935, and phased in over many years, contrasts strikingly to the casualness with which Medicare and Medicaid were added to this system 30 years later. A society that was rich lacked interest in detail, and disdained the efficiency values of the industrial era. Thus, the Congress in 1965 paid little regard to the extreme administrative pitfalls of pouring open-ended funding into a fragmented private health care industry committed to promoting health and longer life.

The Med programs' enactment coincided with the end of a period of stagnation or slow improvement in basic health-status measures, and these programs have operated in a period of unusual gains. Their actual influence on these gains is not clear, but two other facts are:

- o The public has come to regard government as responsible for maintaining a system of ever-higher quality health care; and
- o Costs have escalated so uncontrollably that virtually every institutional and political entity is calling for reform.

Exorbitant medical prices crowd all public priorities. At recent rates of increase, health care would account for 31 percent of Michigan state government total spending by 1990, and 40 percent by 2000. The negative impacts are varied:

o For the uninsured, the explosion of medical costs has created severe hardship. For example, according to a Department of Social Services study, some 9,000 low-income Michigan women annually cover the costs of pregnancy and childbearing without benefit of Medicaid or private insurance.
o For the elderly, higher costs have defeated the original purpose of the Medicare program. Within seven years of Medicare's passage, they were paying more out-of-pocket for medical care than in 1965.
o For the state's businesses, escalating health premiums have compromised competitiveness in the world economy: Chrysler estimates that its medical spending added $600 to the price of a car in 1983.

The clash between public expectations and the medical cost trend is among the most striking legacies of the 1960s. Medical spending has grown much faster than incomes in Michigan. Adjusting for the general inflation rate, this spending jumped from an index of 100 in 1966 to 201 in 1979 and 227 in 1982; meanwhile, per capita income in Michigan rose from 100 in 1966 to 133 in 1979, and fell to 123 in 1982.

The trend for total personal health care spending per capita during the Med programs' first 15 years is shown in Table 5-2 for Michigan and the nation. Again (as with the SI index), Michigan's overall increase roughly matched the national norm, but differences emerge when spending components are separated.

Hospital Care. The state's relatively favorable 15-year trend in spending for hospital care is less impressive in view of its high rate of hospitalization coverage under private insurance before 1966. As a result of Medicare and Medicaid, hospital

SOCIAL AND POLITICAL TRENDS

Table 5-2

U.S. AND MICHIGAN: SELECTED PER CAPITA HEALTH-CARE SPENDING TRENDS

% CHANGE	1966-82	1972-82	1977-82	1981-82
TOTAL				
U.S.	+512%	+227%	+84%	+12%
MICHIGAN	+511	+230	+82	+11
HOSPITALS				
U.S.	+631	+254	+92	+14
MICHIGAN	+598	+270	+92	+12
PHYSICIANS				
U.S.	+463	+226	+84	+12
MICHIGAN	+531	+259	+91	+14
DENTISTS				
U.S.	+449	+213	+76	+12
MICHIGAN	+553	+233	+69	+ 8
OTHER PROFESSIONAL SERVICES				
U.S.	+411	+256	+89	+10
MICHIGAN	+443	+310	+104	+13
DRUGS & SUNDRIES				
U.S.	+242	+117	+51	+ 4
MICHIGAN	+239	+107	+51	+ 4
NURSING HOME CARE				
U.S.	+868	+282	+96	+12
MICHIGAN	+625	+167	+63	+11

PER CAPITA SPENDING (1982 $)	U.S.	MICHIGAN
TOTAL		
1966	$546	$573
1982	1239	1300
HOSPITALS		
1966	216	240
1982	585	622
PHYSICIANS		
1966	129	131
1982	267	306
DENTISTS		
1966	41	42
1982	84	102
OTHER PROFESSIONAL SERVICES		
1966	16	13
1982	31	26
DRUGS & SUNDRIES		
1966	76	82
1982	97	103
NURSING HOME CARE		
1966	33	34
1982	118	92

SOURCE: STATE OF MICHIGAN, OFFICE OF HEALTH AND MEDICAL AFFAIRS.

spending in other parts of the country rose faster than in Michigan, and Michigan's per capita spending excess above national averages dropped 2-3 percent. More recently, it has risen to 6-8 percent. However, the state's greatest cost control weakness has been in professional services. Per capita spending rose from 2 percent above the U.S. level to 15 percent above it; for dentists, the increase was from 2 percent above average to a peak of 25 percent above in 1977-81, with a decline to 21 percent in 1982. These specialists seem to have benefited from the state's general trend toward wage inflation.

Michigan has also lagged in introducing prepaid health maintenance organizations (HMOs). HMOs are one of the few cost-cutting innovations in health care that has shown some ability to combine economy with quality care. But this record does not guarantee that a belated crash program of HMO development would have satisfactory results in the state.

Rapidly escalating costs have encouraged new interest from business and labor in working with government (e.g., through the Economic Alliance) to address the problem. While this reversion to "efficiency thinking" is encouraging, it is operating--in the state as nationally--in a climate of urgency that encourages 1960s-style massive introduction of inadequately tested complex systems. For example, the use of diagnostic categories to determine payments to hospitals under Medicare (and now Michigan's Medicaid) involves, not only an inadequate understanding of hospital costs and weak surveillance capabilities, but a logical incentive for hospitals to reduce average costs within a category by providing lower quality care, by hospitalizing the "least sick" or by discharging the seriously ill too soon.

A different kind of example is the rush to "prudent purchaser" arrangements. Consumer safeguards notwithstanding, the effort to channel ambulatory patients to low-cost providers is subject to abuses, like the Medicaid mills that aroused indignation in the 1970s, by making money on volume, with the quality of care sometimes shockingly poor. A third example is the small but rapidly growing area of home care, where extension to sicker or more disabled patients (those who would formerly have been hospitalized) widens the risks of patient neglect or abuse, and potentially may increase rather than reduce costs.

De-Institutionalization. Reducing hospitalization is a rational objective, since hospitals account for nearly half of Michigan's health-care spending. But de-institutionalization is not necessarily the same as cutting costs. Michigan and the nation have a long standing dislike of hospitals and other large institutions. The emptying of mental hospitals since the introduction of the major tranquilizer drugs in the 1950s has been phenomenal: the number of patients in Michigan's adult facilities dropped from 17,000 in 1960 to about 4,000 in recent years, with a commensurate decline for the mentally retarded since 1965. By 1970, the fashion for de-institutionalization (or "community-based everything") had extended to juvenile misfits, criminals, drug abusers, and the "frail elderly." Although the hope of lower costs was the often cited justification, it was not realized.

If cost control without quality decline is the objective, it is not likely to come from large-scale providers. This is one reason why the substitution of HMOs for solo medical practitioners has won such strong bipartisan support. But "de-hospitalization" generally means more administrative complexity. It can prove a fiasco in the absence of willingness to spend money (and thought and time) to save money and assure orderly progress.

Political Considerations. Fundamental changes in the health care system to control costs cannot be evaluated outside of the broad political consensus that favors saving lives and improving the quality of health care for all Michigan residents. Government is now held accountable for rates of improvement in health-status measures that have recently slowed and, in some instances (e.g., Detroit's infant mortality rate), shown reverses. Many factors besides spending suggest that the strong gains of the 1970s will not continue. Further, the political equation has become harder to read: the most militant champions of high-cost, high-technology medicine to save or protract lives are often conservatives, not liberals.

The broad and powerful coalition of forces supporting cost-control will not endure unless it can demonstrate a strong record of responsible monitoring of medical services with third-party funding. This is difficult, whether one's focus is on profit-motivated providers, on hard-pressed institutions struggling to balance the budget under new rules, or on those whose small-is-beautiful ideology does not include auditors breathing down their necks.

Health Care Prospects. The future? In one scenario, cost-control efforts are discredited by adverse health trends and/or their own deficiencies or failure. The result is another break in continuity, a hastily-designed new national system replacing the Med programs, and possibly extending to the public at large. Even traditional champions of national health insurance do not like this future: they want costs to be controlled first.

In a second scenario, slow but sustained progress reduces the cost spiral, despite some setbacks and scandals along the way. An important question here is whether cost control rejects the 1960s vision of an equal standard of health care for the poor and the rich. This vision is as unrealistic as equal access to mansions and vacations abroad, yet the right to high quality health care seems as basic as the right to high quality education, or to police and fire protection. The implementation of this right through direct governmental provision of medical services was widely discussed early in this century--when the typical physician had little more training and no more income than a career military officer--but it would be enormously difficult to initiate under modern conditions.

Unfortunately, Medicaid's initial "blank check" philosophy of third-party payment has also proved unworkable. High costs severely restrict eligibility; cost-control efforts and red tape reinforce the disinclination of many providers to serve the poor. A successful cost-control scenario may include the return to an open as opposed to a camouflaged "two-tier system," based on the conclusion that quality care for the poor is best assured through new forms of the traditional public clinic.

SOCIAL AND POLITICAL TRENDS

Rationalization of health care, i.e., the appropriate use and payment of labor, seems likely to occur eventually. Although the development of an efficient market for health care has been impeded by explosive spread of the bizarre economics of employment- and government-based third party funding, it will eventually occur in health care, just as it did in earlier goods production.

National consolidation of hospital chains is underway, as is the emergence of competing locally-based health care systems based on HMO or PPO models. Driven by the demands of employees and the leverage of the government and private insurers, control over health care demand is gradually being wrested from doctors and vested in the administrators of these systems. At the same time, experimentation with new delivery mechanisms for many services such as emergency care, outpatient surgery, and diagnostic testing should hasten the development of more efficient health care systems.

While these trends raise heated controversy, they do not raise fundamental ethical issues. By contrast, the question of access to an ever-proliferating array of high-cost life-saving and life-extending technologies raises enormous moral and legal questions. Over the next 20 years, biotechnology will devise economic means to combat some exotic and ordinary causes of premature death. But continuing advances in medical technology do not offer the hope of universal access to the full range of medical procedures. For the indefinite future, the development of a cost conscious, more efficient health care system will force an increasing number of painful moral choices, including not only the right to life and the right to die, but many income based limits on the right to expensive, high technology health care. By 2005, the baby boom generation's retirement will be imminent. The importance of "making haste slowly" in controlling health care costs is underscored by the huge increases in demand that lie just beyond the 20-year outlook.

3. Preserving the Environment: "At What Price?"

Among the attitudes and values of the "urban elites" that have been embraced by the general public, environmental protection has made some of the most striking gains in the past 20 years. Surveys find majorities or pluralities of the public endorsing strong efforts to protect the environment, even at the cost of slower economic growth, higher taxes, or higher automobile prices.

Michigan's role in this trend was evident 20 years ago. The state's exceptional status in water frontage, extent of state lands, forest acreage, and second-home ownership led to broad support for stewardship of the natural environment, based on new values as well as on an older hunting-and-fishing recreational tradition. Further, the heightened concern for health and safety had much to feed on in the state, and still does. Michigan combines the vulnerability of high water tables with the nation's eighth largest production of industrial hazardous waste.[2] Not surprisingly, attitudes in the state have changed greatly since the days when belching smokestakes were proudly featured on its cities' postcards.

In many ways, Michigan's strong environmental ethic is an asset in its quest for durable prosperity. Clean air and water, attractive scenery, access to uncrowded and varied outdoor recreation, and a reputation for vigilance in protecting such assets, can boost the state's competitive standing. Yet there are correlates to the environmental protection movement that pose problems as this movement enlarges its political base.

Productive Use of Land. The first of these correlates bears on the state's ability to dedicate land to its most productive use. The electorate's two-to-one vote to provide constitutional protection for Land Trust revenues is one symptom. Although investing mineral-extraction revenues in the state's long-range future is sound, Michigan already has an exceptional stock of state-owned land. Desirable additions, such as would be supported by the Land Trust, might have been funded by selling off other holdings. If mineral revenues are to

---

[2]Ahead of Michigan in 1983 were Texas, Ohio, Pennsylvania, California, Illinois, Louisiana, and New Jersey. (Congressional Budget Office, *Hazardous Waste Management*, May 1985, p. 22).

SOCIAL AND POLITICAL TRENDS

be invested for the benefit of the state's citizens over the long term, buying up land seems a less logical focus for their use than infrastructure and other economic development investments for localities whose economic base is overly dependent on non-renewable resources.

Not-In-My-Back Yard. A second land use issue is posed by the NIMBYs, the folks who say Not-In-My-Back-Yard to prisons, dumps, housing tracts, businesses, and other facilities that nearly everyone concedes are necessary or desirable somewhere. Preference for keeping familiar surroundings unchanged may not have increased. What is new is the identification of such sentiments with social and civic virtue, and the growth of environmental regulations and procedures that the NIMBYs use with increasing sophistication to obstruct needed development or to delay it and raise its costs.

NIMBYism is more important in some parts of the state than others. On the Upper Peninsula, the traditional forces that have depressed growth--climate, remoteness, and inadequate public investment in infrastructure--are far more important. Elsewhere in the North, the extensiveness of developable territory lets growth flow around "rocks in the river," as one development expert put it. Many northerners realistically accept relative poverty as the trade-off for keeping things as they are. The extent that northern NIMBYism will be an issue for Michigan in the next 20 years depends on and partly controls the degree to which tourism can become a major force in the state's economy.

If Michigan is to realize significant economic benefits from the great increases in leisure and retirement spending that are likely over the next 20 years, the state will need to move much more forcefully to develop its extraordinary natural resources. Such development, even on a more modest scale than has characterized such states as Florida, Arizona, or Nevada, would challenge the values and lifestyles of many Michigan residents. For many, a huge influx of tourist development in order to boost the state's economy would be equivalent to "destroying the village in order to save it." Resolving this conflict is one of the major challenges facing the state.

Michigan resembles New York in the high proportion of its population and production that is packed into a small fraction of its acreage. It is in Detroit, Grand Rapids, and other metropolitan areas that fear or dislike of growth and change have been harmfully reinforced by modern environmentalism. Applying open space and preservationist values to complex industrial metropolitan environments is similar to applying the concept of ecological balance to a cornfield. What Michigan needs--fair and expeditious procedures for settling land use controversies--cannot be gained without a redefinition of the concept of civic responsibility. The key issue is whether proposed land use changes are helpful or harmful to the metropolis. Stopping construction or preventing conversion of a structure from one use to another is sometimes desirable, but it does not stop the clock.

Hostility to growth and change is also salient to the most-mentioned problem of Michigan's environmental efforts: the need for administrative reforms. The Fantus Company's 1982 study for the state concluded: "The overall approach to environmental regulation in Michigan is a cause of serious concern to industry and could impede future growth." The study cited as "commonly held opinions" that the state's Department of Natural Resources and Environmental Protection Bureau were "highly biased, adversarial, and noncommunicative," that the DNR attempts to make law, and that "regulations are not enforced objectively." Also mentioned were serious delays for water, solid waste, and hazardous waste permits--lengthening lead times (and raising costs) for construction.

It is important to appreciate that Michigan's DNR has itself at various times lodged similar objections against the federal EPA for unrealistic standards and costly delays. Like other initiatives rooted in the enthusiasms of the
1960s, environmental regulation suffers from deficiencies of design and from an evangelical fervor that encourages civil servants to be champions of a cause rather than go-by-the-book bureaucrats.

Michigan's potential economic weaknesses make an anti-growth, anti-business reputation especially worrisome. To date, the state has had an advantage in not being plagued by major policy swings such as have occurred on the Potomac. Michigan's commitment to high environmental protection standards can be an asset for economic development objectives.

SOCIAL AND POLITICAL TRENDS

Fair consensus on the basics should mean ability to concentrate on "housekeeping" improvements to build a reputation for evenhanded and timely enforcement procedures. This is important and also fairly likely through "normal" levels of motivation and effort: i.e., it is not nearly so difficult as combatting the attitudinal aspects of NIMBY problems.

Risk Aversion. In addition to anti-change sentiments, the democratization of environmentalism has emphasized reduced toleration of risk. This trend has overlapped with other state policy areas, most notably public health. Industrialization and urbanization have increased public exposure to toxic substances, as well as to hazards associated with congestion and poor sanitation. Meanwhile, increases in affluence and life expectancy have reduced the willingness to accept these hazards--for oneself or others. Government has assumed growing responsibility to protect the home, the workplace, and urban environment.

But influential constituencies have grown even more risk-averse. Generally speaking, post-industrial trends have dramatically broadened individual freedom. The extent to which restrictions on hazardous substances or unhealthy practices will prove an exception to this general rule remains unclear, but the trend is in this direction.

However, it is worthwhile to make a distinction between known and unknown risks. The public tolerates hang-gliders, and it has moved at a snail's pace against tobacco use compared to the militancy of opposition to nuclear power plants. Michigan is not crusading to eliminate the hazard of houses with stairs--but its Department of Public Health has deemed any trace of suspected carcinogens in water as unacceptable if the federal government has not set standards for safe exposure.

Unknowns pose important policy problems. Michigan is measuring many water contaminants unmeasured a decade ago, so that even the direction of their trend is unknown. So are their effects. Consider the case of PCBs. The legislator may read a state-funded study that piles up evidence (almost all from animal research) that standards for Great Lakes fish should be based on a "worst case analysis"--an assumption that any presence of PCBs is a significant health hazard. Yet the legislator may also have seen a recent *Wall Street Journal* editorial asserting that "studies of workers heavily exposed to PCBs found no evidence of ill-health effects even after as much as 40 years of exposure"; that federal statistics show "the number of Americans with high levels of PCBs has already declined sharply," and that public health studies in Michigan and Connecticut show "fish eaters have suffered no known ill effects from PCBs." Moreover, another report to the legislature states that "scientific knowledge about the toxicities of over 65,000 chemical substances in commercial use today is quite limited," thereby raising the question: why single out PCBs?

What should be done? Michigan residents are living longer despite the chemicals to which they are exposed. Were it not for the broad base that environmentalism has acquired, most politicians would be happy to leave it at that. Yet no one can deny that lethal deterioration of the environment *might* occur through long-term buildup of toxicity in the food chain, the soil, groundwater, and human bodies, or through changes affecting heat transfer through the atmosphere, or by means no one has yet discovered. Where risks are fairly well-known, reduced toleration of risk can be combatted with the "99th-percent" argument: i.e., removing the 99th percent of a contaminant from water, air, food, etc., may cost many times more than removing the first 98 percent, with little or no measurable gain. Even here, government is vulnerable to accusations of "putting a price on human life," but this argument can be defused (even where it serves the NIMBYs or other special interests). The unknowns are more problematic. As with the ethical issues of high-tech medicine, science may help to bail the legislator out in the next 20 years, but new forms of the issue will arise. To maximize rational reform of those aspects of environmental policy that are most amenable to common sense approaches is the best strategic goal.

Chapter 6
SOUTHEAST AND OUTSTATE MICHIGAN: A TALE OF THREE CITIES

A. Prospects for Detroit

1. The Roots of the "Urban Crisis"

Because of its unique industrial history, Detroit experienced the bulk of its growth later than most northern cities. Between 1910 and 1930, its population mushroomed from 466,000 to nearly 1.6 million, peaking in 1950 at about 1.8 million. Yet no major northern city began its population decline much earlier than Detroit; none presented a more striking contrast between city straits and metropolitan prosperity; and few had a greater proportional shrinkage than Detroit's 40 percent. In absolute terms, Detroit's population reduction is comparable to the entire 1980 population of Baltimore or Phoenix.

Population losses are nothing new for American cities. Boston at the time of the Revolution was a third smaller than in 1720, owing to industrial decline. Many smaller Midwestern cities experienced shrinkage in the early decades of this century, as a boom based on local natural gas petered out.

The distinction of the postwar urban crisis has been its pervasiveness among the North's largest and hitherto most successful cities. Two major factors were involved. First, these cities lost some of their comparative advantage versus rivals in other regions. Their role as ports weakened and the war spurred growth of population and industry elsewhere. In addition, the drastic decline of foreign immigration--from an annual average of more than a million in 1905-14 to less than 200,000 in 1925-34, and less than 50,000 in 1935-44--nearly destroyed the soft goods manufacturing industries of the North. On the eve of World War I, the foreign-born and their children constituted 75-80 percent of the population of Detroit, New York, Chicago, Boston, and Cleveland. Nevertheless, large cities did better than small ones (and Detroit did spectacularly well) at accommodating to immigration curtailment, and their metropolitan areas dominated northern growth after World War II.

The second key factor of the urban crisis was the cities' own land scarcity. Their era of massive annexations ended early in the century. Although most had suitable vacant land in 1945 to support considerable housing tract development, this was soon exhausted during the postwar building boom. Thereafter, nearly all new construction for middle- and upper-income families with children occurred beyond their bounds.

As is often observed, this trend was also spurred by "white flight" and the automobile, though neither of these factors was really new. Racial and ethnic residential segregation were venerable in American cities. Suburbanization in a socioeconomic (as opposed to jurisdictional) sense had become the dominant choice for middle-income urban families by the 1880s. The advent of electric streetcars in that era initiated the trend toward larger lot sizes; the automobile accelerated that trend. Similarly, inability to redevelop core-area slums or arrest their spread was a prewar urban concern. In this respect, the distinction of the postwar period is not that the blighted area is a larger proportion of the "real" city's acreage--the reverse is true--but that it occupies a rising share of the *jurisdictional* city's territory, generating fiscal problems that compound the initial disability of land scarcity.

Land scarcity is also salient to the prewar and postwar changes in the northern urban economic base. With the waning of soft goods manufacturing, some cities--most notably New York and Chicago--greatly expanded the part of their export economy involving corporate offices and business services. The result was extremely high densities of workers per acre in these cities' downtowns, as well as a high-paid work force and rapid transit systems that fueled suburban sprawl. All these cities have had serious difficulties in the postwar decades. However, their success in establishing logical and profitable uses for their land-scarce urban cores leaves them relatively well-positioned to

SOUTHEAST AND OUTSTATE MICHIGAN

land-scarce urban cores leaves them relatively well-positioned to take advantage of the rapid structural shift of the U.S. economy from manufacturing to services.

Detroit was the most successful city that followed an alternative route to prosperity, basing its ability to support a peak population of nearly two million on the long heavy industry boom. But these industries were space-hungry and often noisy or noxious. Inside as well as outside the city, their locational patterns were decentralized, shaping the location of suppliers, workers' residences, and local commerce. The heavy industry cities--Detroit, St. Louis, Cleveland, Pittsburgh, Buffalo--have experienced the most extreme population declines since 1950. More recently, the straits of basic industry have extended this weakness to the region as well. In 1980-84, four-fifths of the U.S. metropolitan areas that lost population were in the Midwest (including all of Michigan's cities except Grand Rapids), but the relative disadvantage of the core cities has persisted or widened on all available measures.

2. Recent Trends in Detroit

By the mid-1960s, existing plants in Detroit were closing down because they were old, poorly designed for effective use of modern technology, and situated in a deteriorating social environment. Led by the automobile industry, this stagnation and exodus caused the number of manufacturing jobs in the city to level off from the mid-1950s to the mid-1960s, and then to decline precipitously. Total employment paralleled this trend. Through the early 1970s, the suburbs were main beneficiaries, and their growth more than offset Detroit's decline. But since 1973, the slowdown in U.S. and global economic growth and the loss of a sizable fraction of the U.S. automobile market to foreign producers have halted non-cyclical employment growth in the entire metro area.

The city's relative disadvantage has persisted. The proportion of tri-county workers both living and employed in the suburbs rose from 36 percent in 1960 to 62 percent in 1980, while the proportion of suburb-resident workers employed in the city fell from a third to less than a fifth. This occurred in parallel with an extraordinary shift of commerce:

1958-1982

	DETROIT	SUBURBS
No. of Retail Establishments	-11,511	+ 6,215
No. of Retail Jobs	-57,000	+115,000

These statistics imply that a greatly diminished proportion of suburban Detroiters have the urban ties and metropolitan perspective that come from working and/or shopping in the city, while a rising proportion know "their" central city mainly from crime reports on the local news. However, the absolute numbers of suburb-to-Detroit job commuters in the tri-county area declined only from 240,000 to 220,000 between 1960 and 1980, remaining twice the number of "reverse commuters" and equivalent in 1980 to nearly a fifth of the city's resident population. Because Detroit's jobs fell by more than a third in this period, commuters increased their share of these jobs from a third to nearly half. Such data indicate a much higher persistence of city-suburb economic interdependency than the "hole in the doughnut" metaphor suggests. But they also show that a considerable mismatch has developed between the characteristics of the city's own labor pool and the characteristics desired by employers who find a city location preferable or unavoidable.

However this mismatch is construed, its emergence has been linked to racial change. Detroit has become nearly two-thirds black by an unusually extreme process that saw its white population shrink by 1.1 million (73 percent) and its black population increase by 460,000 (153 percent) in thirty years. Even in the 1970s, Detroit city had net in-migration of about 100,000 blacks, although its total population dwindled during the decade by one-fifth. As emphasized earlier, this development was rooted in an inability to accommodate traditional socioeconomic suburbanization--and job development--within city bounds. But the fiscal, political, and social effects of an

SOUTHEAST AND OUTSTATE MICHIGAN

increasingly "underbounded" jurisdictional status generated major new deterrents to city residence and job location for households and businesses that might otherwise have found a Detroit location acceptable or advantageous.

3. Current Issues

Land scarcity as a root cause of Detroit city's problems is becoming a thing of the past. Owing to abandonments, Detroit now has about twelve square miles of vacant land. Its Central Business District (CBD) is strikingly underdeveloped. Although the unrented proportion of its CBD office space is unusually small, the city holds bottom rank among the nation's 33 largest downtowns in the price (per square foot) of office space.

The extreme depression of housing prices is potentially attractive. Detroit has lost more housing than it built every year since 1960; its net loss of 60,000 units in the 1970s was approximated only by New York's Bronx. Yet demand still did not catch up with supply. In 1980, only a handful of the 950 largest U.S. cities had lower median value for their owned homes than Detroit, and the city ranked 709th in median rent. In constant dollars, the value of Detroit's residential property was halved between 1968 and 1983, and the value of its industrial and commercial property dropped by three-fourths.

Providing support for the "hole in the doughnut" metaphor, these statistics are dramatic indicators of the city's failure to manage the challenge of land scarcity well. But this challenge is now shifting to the inner suburbs (and to "suburb-like" neighborhoods in the city). Detroit has new redevelopment potential, based on growing ability to assemble sizable parcels of cleared and clearable land at bargain prices. Unfortunately, strong reasons exist to doubt that this advantage will be effectively exploited before the number of Michigan residents reaching home-buying age shifts from boom to bust in the 1990s.

MICHIGAN BEYOND 2000

4. Fiscal Burdens

The most conspicuous of Detroit's staggering disabilities are frustratingly interrelated: its municipal fiscal burden on solvent citizens and a quality of life that most middle-income families with children will not accept. Detroit's birth rate has shifted from 15 percent below suburban Macomb county's in 1950 to 22 percent above it in 1980. But the particulars are a serious concern:female-headed families with children became 22 percent of all Detroit households by 1980, up from 11 percent as recently as 1970, and compared to 6 percent for the nation at large. Forty percent of all Detroit children are in this disadvantaged situation. A majority are classified as poor; a majority are on welfare, and the city's ADC rolls have increased nearly tenfold.

Detroit's future hinges precariously on upgrading the life chances of these disadvantaged children and on diluting their relative importance in its neighborhoods and schools. Yet public investment to meet this challenge runs up against the fiscal reasons why solvent households continue to flee: bluntly, Detroiters are paying too much for too little. They are paying for public schools to which both black and white parents are unwilling to send their children (enrollment at Detroit's parochial high schools is 43 percent black). They are paying the highest fares in the country for an inferior public transit system that accounts for more than three-fifths of the city's operating deficit, despite heavy federal subsidies whose future curtailment is likely.

Detroiters are also paying--in money as well as anxiety--for a 20-year crime explosion. Although some relative improvement has been registered since the mid-1970s, when Detroit led the nation in its murder, rape, and robbery rates, setbacks continue to occur. Ample reason exists for fear of crime in the streets, property loss, and violence and drugs in the schools. In addition to funding high salaries and fringes for police and fire protection, Detroit has made substantial capital investment in crime reduction: during 1963-83, while its population was dropping by nearly a third, the number of street lights was increased from 62,000 to 85,000 and the number of police vehicles from 946 to 1,646 (although the number of police employees declined slightly).

Because out-migration favors the able, demand for city services does not decline with population, but Detroit's case has been extreme. An American Council on Intergovernmental Relations (ACIR) study of the tax burden for the largest city in each state ranks Detroit first for households with incomes under $25,000, and second to New York for those with $50,000. Reflecting the composition as well as the quantity of out-migration, the city's 1983 income tax rates for individuals and businesses yield in real terms 58 percent of what they would have yielded in 1964. As indicated earlier, the property tax base has also been greatly reduced (with lavish tax abatements skewing the impact).

The 31 percent increase in Detroit's real revenues in 1960-83 came overwhelmingly from state and federal aid. The state-federal share of the city's operating revenues rose from 24 percent in 1960 to about 40 percent in the early 1980s.[1] In addition, potential demands on city government were reduced by enormously increased federal and state outlays for direct provision of income, medical, and other services for the elderly and poor. But this too increased the total tax burden for Detroiters.

5. *The Outlook*

a. Why Worry?

The extremity of Detroit's problems has caused some Michigan residents to adopt the attitude: "If we ignore it, maybe it will go away." In *The Path to Prosperity,* the recent

---

[1]Percentages for many other Michigan cities are comparable, with Grand Rapids topping the list.

report of the Task Force for a Long-Term Economic Strategy for Michigan, neither Detroit nor the general subject of "distressed areas" (defined as troubled cities) is mentioned until page 108 of a 114-page study. Further, the report never refers to the race issue, although there is no doubt that both whites and blacks in the most troubled Michigan metropolitan areas view their problems, policies, and politics in strongly racial terms. Nor does the report deal with the vulnerabilities of the inner suburbs, although they are replicating conditions associated with the onset of urban decay in the past: land scarcity, aging population and physical plant, and lessened locational advantage.

In a state whose population is so heavily metropolitan as Michigan's, it can scarcely be overstated how important the intelligent management of metro evolution is to the 20-year outlook at this time. The interdependency of city and suburbs, and of older and newer suburbs, must soon be recognized as more than a platitude, if the state is to negotiate this difficult period well.

This is most true for the Detroit area, which alone in the state has the population base to support the menu of business and cultural attractions that connotes first-rank metropolitan status. Yet the accessibility problems that accompany great size have entered a new stage. In 1965, an article in the *Detroit Free Press* forecast that helicopters would be as common as automobiles by 1981. Instead, centrally located jobs and amenities are increasingly inconvenient from the land-rich periphery where most new residential construction occurs. Yet this extensive "sprawl" has not raised property values further in--if anything, it has contributed to their depression, raising the possibility that outstaters 20 years hence will refer to the Detroit area not as a doughnut but as a hula hoop.

This raises an unanswerable question: is a hula hoop a viable form for a metropolis of more than 4 million people? Can the services that require such scale be sustained by scattered suburban relocation of traditional city institutions--a Silverdome in Pontiac, business services in Southfield, etc.? Either Michigan residents must cross their fingers and hope that the real and potential advantages accruing to the state from hosting a giant metro market are compatible with the hula hoop configuration or they must give much more thought to devising feasible means for exploiting Detroit's new redevelopment potentialities and recycling its aging commuting suburbs.

b. How Detroit Might Revive

It is easy to base a disaster scenario on the expectation of less financial aid for Detroit--a breakdown of city services, massive exodus by businesses (and by the black as well as the white middle class), population shrinkage to half a million, and major overflow of decay to neighboring jurisdictions. However, it is doubtful that enormous increases in federal aid did Detroit more good than harm in the past 20 years. Instead, these increases skewed political calculations in ways detrimental to the economic base, rendering the management of the city more difficult for its first generation of black leaders.

Stringency is forcing concentration on the economic goals that are necessary if Detroit is to have a future except as a welfare ghetto. This concentration is bearing fruit in the construction of riverfront condos; the close involvement of Strohs, Ford, and ANR in downtown redevelopment; the campaign for regional taxation for the Cobo Hall expansion; and two consecutive years of budget surpluses. But Detroit continues to be held back by ambivalence or hostility toward change. The Synopsis Report of its new masterplan cites a greater concern of its citizens "with preserving their present residential or industrial situation than with instituting major changes, which they fear," and special resistance to land use changes that could cause black dislocations and "gentrification." As in other cities with a drastically eroded economic base, policies that aim to manage retrenchment intelligently are suspect as a white plot to recapture political power.

A durable turnaround for Detroit must begin with recognition that black ascendancy is secure. Under optimistic economic assumptions, the city's population decline will bottom out in the 1990s, with a slight rise to 968,000 by 2005. Of these future

Detroiters, 78 percent will be black.[2] A major influx of young whites is extremely unlikely, considering the state's--and the nation's--demographic outlook at the young-adult ages. Even cities with a record of strong appeal to "gentrifiers"--San Francisco, Boston, Washington--must increase their ability to retain and attract young people if they are not to experience drastic declines in numbers of 25- to 34-year olds. Although Detroit cannot maintain a population near one million without cordiality to white residents, visitors, businesses, and financiers, the principal effect of policies that serve this purpose will be to improve the city's competitiveness with its suburbs (and other cities) for black businesses and the black middle class.

Second, Detroit and Michigan must take heart from the gains blacks have realized. The projection that 53 large American cities will have a "majority minority" population by 2005 has different connotations than it did 20 years ago. As was scarcely imaginable then, the mayors of four of the nation's six largest cities are black, as are the chairmen of five important Congressional committees. Together with rapid growth of the black professional class, a new generation of political leaders is emerging, with a less parochial sense of its constituency, a less abrasive and street-wise political style, and far greater skill at networking and alliance-building. This evolution clearly parallels the urban history of Irish, Italian, and Polish Americans, and it holds great promise for the strengthening of urban governance.

Third, the difficulties that lie ahead require an exciting, inspirational, and credible vision of Detroit's future. This vision has to entail an explicit appeal to racial pride, because it is primarily blacks who must make the sacrifices and efforts to implement it. At least in the first decade of recovery, a key challenge is to "do more with less." Municipal workers must accept much lower rank among the nation's major cities in pay and fringe benefits. Much in the way of service and maintenance that is now done (or not done) by government must be

---

[2]See David McKinney's background paper, *The City of Detroit*, April 1985.

SOUTHEAST AND OUTSTATE MICHIGAN

taken on by civic-minded volunteers. To secure this level of dedication on adequate scale, such a goal as making Detroit "The Capital of Black America" must be promoted in ways that inspire belief and commitment.

Fourth, the goal must be combined with realistic assessment of the outlook. Detroit's employment base is mismatched with its resident labor pool, and its opportunities for growth will perpetuate this mismatch. Through growth and replacement of suburban commuters who retire, Detroit has a chance to enlarge its (mainly black) resident middle class. But it also has the "hula hoop" hazard of losing these jobs to the outer suburbs or to cities (in Michigan or outside it) that still have accessible downtowns. For the time being, the goal of a more prosperous Detroit means fewer Detroiters.

Fifth, Detroit's vision of the future must have a physical dimension. To date, the city has shown itself philosophically averse to land management, turning down HUD's offer to sell its unwanted holdings, and merely collecting parcels for sale if a buyer appears. In 1985, Detroit is passively marketing about 27,000 30' x 100' lots, selling an average of about 1,000 a year. Since the total holdings continue to grow, one cannot speak of a vanishing opportunity. But failure to act has caused abandonment to replace pollution as the city's most serious environmental problem.

Compared to areas like New York's Bronx, Detroit's relatively low population density connotes far greater ease for assembling large parcels of land for planned redevelopment on the exciting scale of true "new towns in town." Construction obviously awaits investor interest, but only political obstacles such as plagued the Poletown project stand in the way of the planning and modeling that could give Detroit's residents a tangible image of what their city may become, and create a momentum that might attract potential redevelopers.

The biggest stumbling block is that Detroit cannot rebuild as it should without uprooting many thousands of mainly poor people. It cannot follow the traditional growth-oriented urban economics that equated "more productive use" of land with higher densities. To retain and attract employed black or white families, the city must seek radical change in a construction ratio of single family houses to apartment units that has recently fallen as low as one to seventy-five (not by anyone's intent but for reasons combining economic depression with the availability of subsidies and marketability considerations). High-rises on the river are fine--perhaps 7,500 more such units will be built by 2005--but their elaborate security arrangements and the predominance of singles and childless couples among their residents illustrate what is wrong more than they point the way to a viable city.

Detroit cannot revive without vastly improved provision of residential settings for worker families with children. As in the suburbs, some of this can be accomplished by facilitating intergenerational turnover of housing in safe, sound neighborhoods: e.g., by encouraging the construction of alternative housing for "empty nest" homeowners, and (with state aid) by reducing financial barriers to home purchase by young families. But this is not remotely sufficient, and little is gained by scatter-site reconstruction in devastated areas with inferior schools and stores. Ironically, the "new town" scale of redevelopment that seems most unrealistic today may hold the best promise for capturing investment, at least as long as slum pathologies are not effectively controlled in the city at large. Certainly there are practical problems of relocating the displaced, but Detroit's exceptional rate of abandonments has reduced these problems to a magnitude that makes bold planning credible. The greater obstacles are short-sighted political calculations and the hostility to change cited in the city's master plan.

Finally, Detroit and its neighbors should consider further regionalization of governmental functions in instances where this promises economies of scale such as those realized by the Detroit area's water system. Negative federal aid developments such as reduced mass transit subsidies will spur this trend. The aging of land-scarce inner suburbs suggests more receptivity to cooperative arrangements: unlike Detroit, many of these jurisdictions have never had a balanced economy. They have played specialized roles in a metropolis whose spatial patterns of growth and decay now threaten to downgrade them. Although their first inclination will be to cooperate (or perhaps even merge) with eachother, specifically racial barriers to closer association with Detroit will dwindle in many cases, because such a high proportion of the potential replacements for their postwar generation of homeowners are black. *Class* barriers can be important even where a major racial transition occurs, but (for better or worse) these city-suburb differences may lessen too.

A wild card in the deck is the substantial amount of Michigan legislation that includes the phrase, "a city having a population greater than 1,000,000..." It would be surprising if Detroit's population does not fall below this magic number by the time of the 1990 Census. The uncertain outcome of the political and legislative processes this statistical event will trigger in Lansing, now creates a disincentive to the "planned shrinkage" strategies that are desirable for Detroit on economic grounds. However, the prospect of a forced reappraisal of the state's hodgepodge of urban legislation could prove timely, if Michigan uses the next few years to develop the factual, analytical, and conceptual basis for legislators to make metropolitan policy decisions that serve the state's interests.

B. Grand Rapids

The Grand Rapids metropolitan area helps to dispel the preconceptions that many of those who live outside Michigan have about the state. Rather than having been overwhelmed by economic, social, and technological change, the people and institutions of Grand Rapids have learned to adapt and benefit from it.

As a result, Grand Rapids has done better than the state as a whole in employment and population growth during the 1970s and even during the turbulent years of the last recession. From 1970 to 1980, Kent County grew by 8.1 percent, almost double the statewide growth of 4.4 percent. The county grew another 4.5 percent by 1984, reaching a total population of 461,000, at a time when the state experienced a significant population loss. While the Grand Rapids area was significantly affected by the last recession, its unemployment rates have remained lower than the average statewide. As of mid-1985, wage and salary employment stands at a record 282,000. In part, this is because the area's manufacturing economy has rebounded more strongly than the rest of the nation; manufacturing jobs at the end of 1984 numbered 13,000 more than at the end of 1982. Substantial growth has also occurred in the nonmanufacturing sector during that time period.

1. Economic Adaptation

One example of a successful economic adaptation in Grand Rapids involves the transition of the city from a center of production of fine wood furniture into a major producer of metal office furniture. The wood furniture industry grew up in Grand Rapids, largely because of the availability of inexpensive, high quality lumber produced by the mills in the area. As the availability of furniture-grade lumber declined, so did a significant portion of the area's wood furniture production. That decline has been more than offset, however, by growth in the metal furniture industry. This transition, which combined the furniture design and marketing skills available in the wood furniture industry with the metal forming and manufacturing skills available in the auto industry, was not simply good luck. It depended on the insight, intelligence, and hard work of many Grand Rapids residents.

This is not an isolated example. The concerted effort being made to turn Grand Rapids into a regional center for convention and tourist business isanother case of an attempt to anticipate significant changes (in this case the overall national decline of manufacturing and the increase in leisure time) and to find viable alternatives for generating wealth. As is the case in other successful midwestern cities such as Columbus, Ohio, and Indianapolis, the people of Grand Rapids seem to have learned to work together to manage change.

2. Cooperation Between Jurisdictions

An important characteristic of Grand Rapids that has contributed to its relative success in coping with change has been the cooperation among civic jurisdictions in the metropolitan area. The city of Grand Rapids has almost no land available for industrial growth. Surrounding communities, such as Kentwood and Wyoming, do have space available. Development in Grand Rapids city has, therefore, been consciously directed toward improving the city's ability to supply such services as shopping, entertainment, cultural amenities, public services, transportation, and communications. It has also been directed toward the development of tourism and convention business, and regional business services. The surrounding communities have concentrated on industrial growth and residential construction. It was probably difficult for city officials to accept the notion that the growth of the city was being physically constrained and that the direction of development had to change as a result. Nevertheless, they and officials in surrounding communities have created a cooperative strategy for dealing with this change that seems to be working to the benefit of the entire metro area. While this cooperation is far from perfect, it has worked well enough to promote both a surprisingly high quality of life and a reasonable degree of economic opportunity for residents of the area.

3. Political Leadership

The political leadership of the area has also apparently been successful in forging a strong alliance with the area's business leaders. Unlike several neighboring cities, Grand Rapids has no single corporation that dominates its economy. It is home to several large companies (for example, AMWAY, Herman Miller, Keeler Brass, Steelcase, Wolverine Worldwide, among others), as well as a second tier of somewhat smaller firms. These local companies are major employers and contributors to the economy of the area. Many have also committed resources and personnel to the development efforts taking place.

Most of these cooperative efforts have been undertaken on an ad hoc basis rather than as part of a consensus plan, but the system that has evolved seems to work reasonably well. This "system," if such a word can be used to describe the loose and variable coalition of political and business leaders in Grand Rapids, would be hard to describe, define, and replicate. But it is precisely this looseness that seems to make it acceptable to many participants. Other political and corporate leaders in Michigan might look to the Grand Rapids model as one from which they could learn ways to cooperate constructively.

MICHIGAN BEYOND 2000

4. Cost Factors

Other more easily quantifiable factors also contribute significantly to the economic vitality of the region. Worker's compensation costs are lower in the Grand Rapids area than in the Detroit region, and medical costs are apparently among the lowest in the Great Lakes region. Property tax rates are also below the state average. These and other cost factors, including average wage rates, contribute to the attractiveness of Grand Rapids as an alternative to the southeastern area of the state for manufacturers considering a Michigan location.

Another factor that contributes to the attractiveness of the area from a business standpoint is a sense that local problems are manageable and are being addressed competently. For example, the housing stock is in generally very good shape. The principal area in need of rehabilitation is a small section on the city's near southeast side, and city government has apparently begun to address the problem effectively. There exists no discernible sense that the city of Grand Rapids is likely to confront any problem that is beyond its resources or capabilities. As a result, the business community seems to perceive Grand Rapids as a relatively risk-free, stable, and congenial place for investing and operating.

This perception of stability may not be completely warranted. Though the area's economy is much less dependent on a single industry than those of many other Michigan cities, it is still highly concentrated in manufacturing, with almost a third of all jobs in the area in that sector. About 70 percent of manufacturing jobs are in durable goods production, a proportion slightly lower than the state as a whole. Most disturbing of all is that the largest single employer in the area is General Motors, which employs up to 9,000 workers in three plants. In addition, many smaller firms rely on the auto industry for much or all of their business. As a result, Grand Rapids continues to be very sensitive to economic downturns. Moreover, it is likely that auto-related employment (though not auto-related output) will fall significantly over time. Business and government leaders in the area must remain aware of this prospect and be constantly on the lookout for development opportunities that will allow them to wean themselves away from dependence on the auto industry, particularly if those opportunities also involve reducing the area's concentration in durables manufacturing.

A favorable business cost climate (relative to other Michigan locations), cooperation among governments and between government and business, natural and cultural amenities, and a variety of other factors can result in a period of sustained growth for the Grand Rapids area for the next two decades. Net employment growth in the region is likely to be at about the national average, approximately one percent per year, over that period. Grand Rapids will be faced with a long-term structural adjustment, as a result of its current concentration in autos and related businesses, but it is better positioned to manage that structural change than virtually any other area in the state.

C. Traverse City

Compared to Detroit or even to Grand Rapids, the Traverse City area might seem to be relatively unimportant to Michigan's future. The ten-county area around Traverse City contains only a small fraction of the state's employment and population, and Traverse City itself does not even appear in the list of the twenty largest cities in the state.

But, because it is the state's leading tourist destination, the Grand Traverse Bay area, and other areas like it in the upper Lower Peninsula, will have much more impact on the future of Michigan than these numbers imply. Not only will these areas grow rapidly over the next two decades, thereby increasing their economic and political influence, they also symbolize the lifestyle and the economy toward which Michigan is trending. With an employment base built less on manufacturing than on services and tourism, and with public priorities strongly influenced by "post-industrial values," the Traverse Bay area offers a glimpse of how Michigan's population and economy are likely to change between 1985 and 2005.

Throughout its history, Traverse City's economy has depended on natural resources. The timber industry of the late 1800s was followed by an agricultural one based largely on orchards. At an accelerating pace during the twentieth century, economic growth has developed around another key resource: water and scenery. With a geography dominated by rolling green hills and thousands of miles of sandy beaches lining the shores of Lake Michigan and many smaller lakes, Traverse City has been a resort center for decades. As tourism boomed in the post-World War II era, the area's attractiveness has led to spectacular population gains. After adding residents at an average rate of 15 percent per decade through most of the twentieth century, the Traverse City area grew by more than 30 percent from 1970 to 1980. Although the 1980-1982 recession caused a temporary pause in this upward trend, it appears to have resumed recently.

1. Who Lives in Traverse City?

As the leading tourist area in the state, the Traverse City area is quite different from the rest of Michigan. Its population is more likely to have moved to the area from outside the region, and these migrants are concentrated among the young and old. In 1980, for example, more than a third of the residents of Grand Traverse and Kalkaska counties had lived there less than five years--double the proportion in the rest of the state. From 1970 to 1980, the numbers of people aged 20 to 34 in the ten counties surrounding Traverse City grew by some 85 percent, more than twice the growth for the rest of the state. Over the same time period, those over 65 increased by 41 percent, again twice the statewide rate.

The region's employment base is also far different from that elsewhere in Michigan. Manufacturing, for example, employs only 16 percent of the workforce, compared to 26 percent for the state as a whole. Services (excluding government) provide 64 percent of the jobs, compared to 54 percent for all of Michigan.

Traverse City and similar areas in Michigan are likely to grow rapidly over the next two decades. Three trends may play a major role in this growth: the development of large new resorts and convention centers, the growth in the number of individuals reaching retirement age, and the expansion of jobs in

SOUTHEAST AND OUTSTATE MICHIGAN

service industries, particularly those in research, development, and engineering.

2. Retirees

Of these trends, the growth of the retiree population is the most certain and the most beneficial to the area. Between 1980 and 2000, the number of Michigan residents over the age of 65 will increase by 23 percent. Many of these older residents will pick Michigan's lakefront areas as the place for their retirement. They may be joined by large numbers of somewhat younger Michigan residents who will choose (or be forced) to retire in their mid or late 50s. In particular, the reductions projected in automobile industry employment are likely to result in substantial waves of retirement among both blue and white collar workers as one way of "downsizing" the work force. The income of these retirees will be of major importance in supporting the growth of areas such as Traverse City. Just as the boom in retirement communities in Florida and Arizona led to subsequent growth in retailing, construction, health care, and many other service industries, a swelling population of retirees in Traverse City and similar resort communities in Michigan will generate strong service based economic growth.

3. Tourist and Industrial Development

Less certain, but also of potential importance to the area, will be the growth of large scale tourist and convention facilities. Until recently, most of the tourist development that occurred in the Traverse City area was small-to-medium scale facilities with relatively few amenities. Grand Traverse Resort, with its elaborate golfing, swimming, tennis, convention, and shopping facilities, is a major departure from this pattern. Although the success of this facility is uncertain, the stage seems set for rapid proliferation of similar large scale resorts. Gradual improvements in air and highway access to the area from the Detroit and Chicago metropolitan areas will help to reinforce this trend. As the numbers who visit Traverse City's resorts grow, more high quality services and facilities will be developed to serve them, triggering a cycle of self-perpetuating growth.

The Traverse City area may also benefit from the development of new high technology research and development facilities. Although there is currently little such employment in the area, the potential for establishing new facilities of this type is significant. Increasingly, improvements in communications and transportation are making it possible to locate corporate facilities, such as headquarters buildings, education or training centers, or R&D laboratories, wherever attractive living and working conditions are found. With some of the most pleasant and scenic sites in the state, Traverse City could potentially attract such corporate facilities much more easily than it could win traditional manufacturing plants. This could be especially true if the community decided to concentrate on attracting such facilities.

4. Growth Projections

Even without explosive growth of large resorts or aggressive pursuit of high technology corporate facilities, the Traverse City area can expect substantial growth over the next 20 years. In contrast to the state as a whole, which is not expected to show any significant population gains over the next two decades, the Traverse City area is likely to experience growth of at least 3 percent per year. By the year 2005, this growth rate would boost the population of the ten county area from the current 215,000 to approximately 388,000, almost doubling its share of the state's population to more than 4 percent. The major uncertainty in this projection, and the central policy issue facing the area's residents, is whether such growth will be encouraged or even permitted. To many people, both long-time residents and newcomers, growth on such a scale threatens the values and the lifestyle that they prize most. While there is no inherent limit on the population density that a given resort area can sustain (e.g., Florida's east coast), rapid growth in the Traverse City area will certainly change, and for some will spoil, its current unhurried, cottages-by-the-lake ambience. How this issue is resolved by the residents of the area, and whether how quickly the Traverse City region will grow.

128

Chapter 7
MICHIGAN 2005:
THREE PERSPECTIVES ON THE FUTURE

Looking back from the perspective of 2005, Michigan's evolution during the last years of the twentieth century will seem to have been almost inevitable. The forces acting on the state--international competition, the changes in manufacturing technology, the aging of the population, and the loss of federal aid--will have combined to produce a result that most observers will assume could not have been otherwise.

But looking ahead from 1985, Michigan's future seems far less certain. Although some forces are unpredictable, such as the rate of national economic growth, and some policies are beyond Michigan's control, such as the rules governing international trade, the state *can* shape its future.

What follows are three perspectives on possible Michigan futures. One is a summary of the fundamental trends and factors drawn from the preceding analysis: the "standard world" or "surprise-free" scenario.

The second is a more far-reaching, and in some ways more exciting, future in which technology has blossomed to create an automated, leisure-oriented, post-industrial society in the state. Although some of the technological possibilities of the scenario may seem surprising, all fall within the realm of possibility within the next twenty years.

The third scenario combines a much less sanguine national economic climate with a mix of different decisions and non-decisions at the federal and state level, leading to radically different outcomes. In this recession-driven scenario, Michigan decisionmakers face the most wrenching, divisive issues of stagnant growth and lost competitiveness.

These scenarios are not predictions and they are not mutually exclusive. Aspects of each scenario may occur simultaneously. They are meant to be visions of the future that provoke thought and illustrate possibilities. They are intentionally written from different perspectives, to stretch thinking about how the future might be shaped. Because concerned, reasonable people usually find ways to promote their best interests, the future is most likely to resemble the revitalized, technologically advanced Michigan of the "standard world." But any of the outcomes is possible.

A. Michigan 2005--A "Surprise-Free" Scenario

How do all of the trends and forces affecting Michigan fit together? What will Michigan be like in the next century? Despite the obvious uncertainties of such a distant horizon, these are some of the most likely outcomes over the next twenty years:
oThe Michigan economy will continue to grow steadily, pulled along by a strong U.S. economy. But, in contrast to overall national economic performance that is projected to grow at slightly more than 3 percent annually during the period 1985-2005 (compared to 2.9 percent from 1965 to 1985), Michigan is likely to expand at only about 2.5 percent per year. The state will suffer more severe recessions than the nation as a whole, and per capita income will remain below the national average.

> o *Michigan will continue to be a major manufacturer of automobiles, "smart" industrial tools, and associated products.* Startling advances in the capabilities of robots and other automated manufacturing systems, especially those employing machine vision, advanced sensors, and "artificial intelligence" will have enabled many Michigan firms to remain on the leading edge of manufacturing technology. At the same time, a combination of yen-dollar revaluations and/or continued import restraints on Japanese vehicles will have kept the Japanese share of U.S. motor vehicle sales

from rising above 35 percent. This retention of manufacturing infrastructure and capabilities will promote further rapid growth of service industries, ranging from accounting and computer programming to retailing and restaurants.

o *Despite the continued importance of manufacturing as an anchor for growth, manufacturing employment will not increase, particularly in traditional assembly line occupations.* Even if auto sales grow steadily, and markets for other Michigan products such as office furniture or robots expand rapidly, employment in manufacturing will remain stable at just over 1 million. In Michigan, as in the rest of the country, highly-automated manufacturing plants will produce more with fewer workers. In the automobile industry, for example, half as many workers will be needed to produce the same number of vehicles. Employment in service industries will have climbed rapidly, however, more than making up for the stagnant level of factory jobs. By 2005, more than three-fourths of the jobs in Michigan will be service jobs. There will be more people working in the finance, real estate, and insurance businesses than in auto manufacturing.

o *As manufacturing jobs shrink, the skills required of the remaining workers will rise rapidly.* The average production worker in the year 2005 will need to understand mathematics and statistics, the use of computers, and basic engineering concepts.

o *Fewer people will live in the state.* Increases in births and immigration will not fully counterbalance outmigration, so that the state's population will shrink slightly, both absolutely and relative to the rest of the country. On average, those living in Michigan are likely to be older, with the largest increases coming among those age 45-60. In the redistricting following the year 2000 census, Michigan will emerge with only 15 representatives in Congress.

MICHIGAN BEYOND 2000

o *Michigan's residents will be much more dispersed across the state than they are today.* Much of the state may experience a boom, while Detroit and some of its near-in suburbs languish. As a result, many fewer people will live and work in Detroit and its near-in suburbs, and many more will reside in the far exurbs of Detroit, and around the cities of Kalamazoo and Grand Rapids. If current trends continue, by the year 2005 there will be more people living in the Grand Rapids SMSA (Kent and Ottawa counties) than remain in the city of Detroit.

o *Black people, particularly those living in Detroit, will face the greatest difficulties as a result of the changes in Michigan's economy.* Every change that Michigan can expect--the relative decline of factory wages and the loss of factory jobs, the cutbacks in federal support, the need for better-educated workers, and the continuing erosion of Detroit--will hurt blacks worse than whites. Detroit--which will be almost four-fifths black by 2005--will face a continuous cycle of fiscal crisis.

o *A much smaller share of state and local budgets will be funded by federal programs.* The state will be forced to rely more on its own tax base and to take more responsibility for regulating business activity.

o *Detroit's cycle of decay is likely to have begun to turn around by 2005.* Rebuilding outward from a core of development along the riverfront and relying during the early stages to a great degree on its own resources, the black community of Detroit will have gradually begun to turn the city and its institutions around. Black leaders who are independent of legislators in Lansing and Washington, not patient with racism as an explanation for problems and more willing to challenge the old political rules and their own constituency, will initiate the revitalization. Though early progress will be slow, the direction should be unmistakable by the year 2005. Meanwhile, the trends in near-in suburbs, with aging populations, rapid racial changes, and declining tax bases, may have become the focus of concern.

These surprise-free projections of a more exurban, white collar, bettereducated, high-tech Michigan depend on a number of relatively optimistic assumptions. But if the economy should return to its recession/inflation prone pattern of the 1970s, Michigan would be much worse off. If import restraints are eliminated, Japanese auto imports could increase well above their predicted 35 percent share of the U.S. market. If Japanese auto assembly plants in the U.S. grow rapidly, GM, Ford, and Chrysler plants in Michigan could close. If service employment does not grow at the rapid pace anticipated, unemployment in the state will remain at recession levels indefinitely, leading to sustained out-migration. *Many of the uncertainties in Michigan's future are downside risks. Achieving this relatively optimistic outcome in the surprise-free scenario requires both good luck and good management.*

B. Post-Industrial Michigan--The Information and Leisure Society

Another perspective on Michigan in the year 2005 emphasizes the explosion of technology underway in the state and elsewhere across the country. This future is driven by astounding, but not impossible, advances in computers, communications, and leisure and by bold steps taken by the state to exploit the new possibilities.

For a glimpse of how this post-industrial Michigan might look, there is no better place to begin than inside an automobile assembly plant. Our hypothetical facility, which was built by an American company outside of Grand Rapids in 1993, has just undergone its first total renovation and now represents the state-of-the-art in automobile manufacturing.

The complex is in operation around the clock, but most of the few hundred technicians needed to operate the plant are present only between 9:00 a.m. and 3:30 p.m., when the assembly line is halted for maintenance. During the night and through the weekends, the plant operates in unheated semi-darkness with relentless, automated efficiency. Only a few work teams are present to monitor the tools and make emergency adjustments or repairs. Virtually every operation--from materials handling to assembly and quality monitoring--is in the hands of one of the newest generation robots. These machines, which were developed in state-funded research centers in Ann Arbor, can not only see and "feel" with superhuman accuracy, they can inspect each part as it passes through their hands, make adjustments in response to variations in parts or vehicle styles, and communicate with the plant's central computer.

Although many of the jobs in the plant involve familiar skills--repair of electronic and hydraulic equipment, for example--the most striking difference between these workers and their predecessors twenty years earlier is the complete absence of unskilled trades. Even the least-educated workers have taken several years of math, statistics, electronics, and engineering courses. Under the company's continuing education program, half-funded by the state, every worker is encouraged to return to school periodically to update and upgrade his skills.

Let us follow one of the plant's engineers as he heads for home at the end of his shift. To outward appearances the car he climbs into resembles those of twenty years before, although it is plastic-skinned and more aerodynamically shaped that its predecessors. But once on the road, the differences become apparent. When the engineer reaches the interstate, he switches on his car's "autoguide" feature, which enables him to take his eyes off the road and his hands off the wheel while his car drives itself. "Autoguide" is a still- experimental system that was developed as a cooperative venture between the U.S. and Michigan Departments of Transportation and the Motor Vehicle Manufacturers Association. It combines some of the technologies in the robots the engineer works on--machine vision and sophisticated sensors--with satellite and radio navigation systems, and roadside location markers. Together, these devices enable the engineer's car to proceed along the main highway without his attention, slowing or stopping in response to traffic and then resuming speed.

This revolutionary system has just begun to become available across the country, as state highway departments equip their roads for automatic traffic and the automakers offer the expensive, optional system to customers. Because the engineer works for an auto company, he was one of the first to install the system and to take advantage of the new opportunities it made possible.

Those opportunities are remarkable. For example, this engineer has chosen to live on Traverse Bay, two hours to the north of Grand Rapids, despite the long drive, because he can use the travel time productively. In the morning, he spends the first hour reading the morning paper (delivered electronically to his car via satellite), then spends the second watching a lecture and answering questions for the accounting class he is taking this semester, as part of his effort to finish his MBA. In the evening he can "report" to a second job, a part-time telephone sales position with an insurance company, without ever leaving his car. Using his car phone and the computer built into his car, he can call selected individuals across the state, discuss their financial needs, offer them a variety of policy choices, and arrange for contracts to be mailed to their homes, without putting pen to paper or slowing down.

This evening, he "leaves work" early to shop for a housewarming present for a friend moving in near his home. After browsing through an on-line catalog, he selects a small kitchen appliance. Switching to another database, he locates a warehouse outlet near his home that has an attractive price and can guarantee delivery by the weekend, when the housewarming party will take place. With his credit card and a few keyed instructions, he completes his purchase. Just before he takes control of his car again to leave the interstate, he places one last call--to a local pizza parlor, requesting that his dinner meet him at home in fifteen minutes.

The area in which this engineer lives, and many others along the western and southern shores of the Lakes, has experienced explosive growth over the last ten years. This growth has been fueled not only by growing numbers of very long distance commuters but by decisions by a number of high-technology research, marketing, and engineering firms to relocate their headquarters to these areas. Drawn by the pleasant surroundings and high levels of amenities, these new facilities are tied to their markets or home offices by cheap, high-capacity data, voice and video communications links and by rapidly improving air service. The first to take advantage of the possibilities were the huge programming and automation engineering staffs of the automobile companies that were relocated to lake shore complexes during the mid-1990s. Once this nucleus of industry was in place, dozens and then hundreds of similar firms soon followed, and growth accelerated as service industries such as health care, retailing, and construction expanded to serve the new residents. At the same time, the tourist industries that were the economic mainstays of the area have also leap-frogged ahead, with huge new convention facilities, resorts, and amusement parks sprouting up in the region.

Across the state, in the western suburbs of Detroit another high tech industry has blossomed: home robots. One firm in particular, General Robotics, or GR as it has come to be known, dominates the industry.

From its beginnings in the kitchen of a doctoral student's suburban Detroit home, GR has grown to become one of the premier industrial companies in the world. Few of its factories have more than minimal human labor force, of course, since General Robotics employs both its own general purpose robots and the heavy industrial robots manufactured by his competitors. But the company employs almost a quarter of a million people worldwide, over half of them in Detroit, in research and development, design, marketing, and similar activities. General Robotics has played an important role in shoring up the Michigan economy in the early years of the twenty-first century.

Why did GR grow so rapidly in Michigan? The founder was a Michigan resident. Early in its history, the firm received substantial venture capital funding and contracts from a

MICHIGAN 2005

Michigan auto maker. Although the market for the machines soon became national, and GR now hires engineers from across the nation, the headquarters has remained in the state.

The breakthrough that took robots out of the auto factories and into homes occurred in the late 1990s. In a video tape that has subsequently been replayed thousands of times, a twenty-eight year old doctoral student in engineering stands before a sink filled with sudsy water. He holds in front of him a fine crystal goblet, an arm reaches out from the haphazard pile of electronics and mechanical linkages sitting next to him on a motorized wheel chair. The strange collection of equipment actually represents a synthesis of new generalized programming techniques, advanced tactile sensing technology, and a very sophisticated new vision system. The arm grasps the goblet and dunks it in suds. A second arm sponges the goblet, turns on the water to rinse it, and then towels it dry. The robot holds up the goblet to its own face to inspect it, then offers it to the human being. Admiring the handiwork of his mechanical protege, the man utters the famous phrase, "If it can do this, it can also do windows."

"It can also do windows" since became one of the most successful advertising slogans in history. The phrase is not only literally true, it illustrates the enormous advances in these machines. Robots are now trusted to do almost every conceivable household chore, including the delicate and tedious tasks that in the past were difficult even to hire out. Of course, today's robots bear little resemblance to the collection of odd pieces first assembled. Nor do they resemble the humanoid monstrosities of twentieth century science fiction. Instead, they probably resemble nothing so much as a garbage can on rollers, with the can housing memory, "brain," sensors, and other essentials. Specialized arms, grippers, and other attachments can be added, which allow them to wash dishes, do the laundry, vacuum, dust, mix drinks, serve canapes, walk the dog...and of course, do windows.

Though this fanciful scenario may seem to be too good to be true, it is not likely to be free of controversy or debate within Michigan. First, and most importantly, the geographic freedom that advanced transportation and communications systems might bring to individuals and firms does not guarantee that Grand Rapids or Traverse Bay or any other community in Michigan will benefit. Although these areas are certainly attractive, and are the most likely in the state to gain, the competition for people and economic activity will be national and global. The five thousand robots and five hundred technicians needed to make cars can be moved to Kentucky as easily as to Kalamazoo. No technology will save Michigan from the need to be competitive.

Second, rapid growth outside southeast Michigan is likely to exacerbate the long-standing tensions between Detroit and outstate Michigan, and between pro-growth and anti-growth forces within the state. With every orchard that is swallowed to make way for a new subdivision, the concerns over urban sprawl will mount. At both the local and the state level, a high-tech, more deconcentrated Michigan is likely to be a turbulent Michigan. If Michigan is extremely successful at developing its high technology base, many within the state will warn against repeating the "mistakes" of Silicon Valley in the development of "Automation Alley" or other new areas. And to the degree that many of the firms and individuals that settle in such high growth areas come from the older areas of Michigan, there will certainly be criticism from the unfavored areas that the new ones are unfairly stealing people and jobs.

Finally, technology will threaten many of the institutions and organizations that currently hold sway in Michigan. A world in which high quality information and education could be delivered electronically to homes, offices, or cars is a world in which traditional educational institutions would adapt much different roles. Not only might colleges and universities have to specialize to a greater degree, they might find themselves competing with cheaper, non residentially-based institutions for students and professors. At the elementary and secondary level, public schools that fail to adapt to the technology might find themselves in competition with many new private or corporate alternatives that would deliver high quality education to the home or neighborhood center. At all levels of education, the teacher's role will shift dramatically from that of lecturer and information provider, to that of discussion leader, advisor, and computer manager.

None of the debates or policy challenges of this scenario are as difficult or challenging as those that stem from less fortuitous circumstances. For Michigan, high-technology growing pains would be minor annoyances compared to the hardships of an economic calamity.

C. Michigan Tested: Dealing With Another Deep Recession

This scenario begins with what many consider to be an almost inevitable event: another severe recession. Like the recession that began in 1980, this one causes a deep, prolonged slowdown of auto sales, and huge job and income losses throughout Michigan. And like the 1980 recession, this one brings calls for restraints on Japanese car imports, to which the Japanese, sensitized by their continuing trade frictions with the U.S., respond almost immediately, cutting back their current quota by 10 percent and freezing it indefinitely at the new lower level.

At first, these events trigger only the by-now-familiar series of events common to all recessions. Across the state, workers and governments tighten their belts. As the unemployment lines lengthen, spending increases are cut, vacations and new purchases postponed, and a gritty, wait-it-out attitude develops.

A year and a half later, just when the first signs of hope begin to emerge, a new crisis develops. As the recession reaches other developed nations, the U.S. dollar, which had been falling, begins to strengthen. A number of developing countries, whose debts are denominated in dollars, find that, with the recession weakening their exports to the U.S. and other developed nations, they cannot meet their obligations. Three South American countries simultaneously announce that they will suspend all debt and interest payments until further notice.

MICHIGAN BEYOND 2000

This default triggers a run on two major U.S. banks. Although immediate action by the Federal Reserve averts a full scale panic, the banking system is deeply shaken, and consumer confidence is undermined. The U.S. plunges even deeper into the recession.

In Michigan, the already-grim conditions lurch toward crisis. The Japanese automakers have responded to the import restraints by returning to the strategy of exporting only the largest, most option laden vehicles under the restraints, and by announcing large additions to their domestic production capacity. Some analysts are projecting that, within five years, the Japanese will be able to produce 3 million vehicles in North America, up from the current 1 million. Since most of these vehicles will be produced in new, lowerwage plants outside of Michigan, domestic companies facing steep losses and a long-term erosion in the most profitable part of their market request a new round of labor negotiations aimed at reducing wages and eliminating work rules. The UAW, whose objective had been to bring the new plants of offshore producers up to the standards of the national contract, instead finds itself under pressure to reduce wages and relax standards down to the lowest common denominator.

In the Detroit area, three large assembly plants close, throwing the city and many suburban jurisdictions into deep financial trouble. The exodus from Detroit and Michigan, which had slowed markedly during the previous recovery, returns to a flood. The most able and the most educated depart, leaving behind more recipients of welfare and other social programs. Detroit undertakes several rounds of layoffs, but the squeeze gets steadily worse. Unable to obtain state or federal assistance, the city is faced with receivership.

The state government, too, is in a deep financial bind. Rather than cut taxes and expand spending, the choices suddenly include only budget cuts and tax increases. Other policy goals are ignored, in a desperate effort to keep the state afloat.

This scenario has more than one logical ending. It is often said that democracies cannot act decisively, except in crisis. For Michigan, the central question during another deep recession would be whether the state's decision-makers could act boldly enough not merely to weather the crisis but to benefit from it. If the state could act decisively, it could expect to emerge from these difficulties stronger than before. If it did not, the recession could become part of a sustained decline.

How might these different outcomes occur?

1. Michigan Eclipsed: The Price of Inaction.

In a pattern reminiscent of earlier years, the efforts by business and labor, the political parties, and urban and suburbanites to find mutually beneficial solutions to the crisis break down. Although Detroit offers a range of accommodations and alternatives in an attempt to find solutions to its problems, neither the state nor the federal government is willing to lend much help. Historic rivalries and suspicions between blacks and whites not only block bold steps, but almost prevent any action at all. Finally, a patchwork aid program is cobbled together that allows the city to limp through the recession with further deep cuts in services and an additional long-term debt burden.

The state budget encounters a similar logjam. Efforts to preserve education spending and other programs that could benefit the state in later years are defeated, in part because of partisan jockeying. Capital spending programs are slashed, but all other program cuts are made on a formula basis, with certain social spending exempted. Tax increases, which had been forsworn by both parties a year earlier, are finally legislated.

The labor negotiations, conducted in an atmosphere of unspoken threat to move production to plants where workers agree to the givebacks, turn into a deadlock. Although the contract is of vital interest to the state's future, most state leaders not directly involved refrain from commenting, much less suggesting, that the state government might participate in some way in helping to find a solution. After a brief bitter strike, a new contract is signed that trims wages and relaxes work rules on a national basis. But the agreement is not sufficient to make Michigan plants fully competitive with those of Japanese producers elsewhere in the country, and all of the domestic manufacturers begin making quiet plans to move production to new locations further south, to be competitive with the Japanese plants. Over the next six years, Michigan's share of automobile production is cut in half.

2. Michigan Strengthened by Adversity

The atmosphere of crisis in another deep recession might set off an entirely different set of reactions, leading to fundamental realignments and collective action to strengthen the state's competitive position. Under this outcome, the gravity of the situation leads to a willingness by leaders of all stripes to consider new possibilities.

Negotiations between the state, the city of Detroit, and its suburbs lead to far reaching agreements for reshuffling responsibilities, bureaucracies, and tax burdens. In return for state assistance with its fiscal crisis, the city and Wayne County agree to joint administration of some services and consolidation of others. A new basis for sustained cooperation is established.

In the capital, the impasse over the budget cuts is finally broken when a bipartisan group of legislators, meeting in secret, manages to design a package that commands support from the leadership of both parties. Education and capital investment programs are spared deep cuts, as the state finds ways to trim non-essentials. The fragile alliance survives the recession and becomes the basis for reshaping state budget priorities over the next several years.

At the bargaining table, union and management leaders, urged on by leaders from state government, sign a historic agreement that provides union locals with the autonomy to agree to wage and workrule givebacks in return for new investments in modernization and profit-sharing on an unprecedented scale. While there is grumbling in both the union halls and on Wall Street, the agreement leads to spectacular cost improvements in many Michigan plants, and, when the recession ends, forms the basis for a strong revival of Michigan's industry.

Although it would be comforting to believe that a crisis caused by another deep recession will bring out the best in

Michigan institutions, an analyst would clearly be more inclined to bet on Michigan Eclipsed rather than Michigan Strengthened as the outcome of this scenario. The 1980 recession was not as deep as the one posited here. But many of the decisions made over the last five years do not appear to have been aimed at enhancing Michigan's long-term competitiveness or to have focused on the need for collective action to achieve it. Michigan has become so confident that every recession will have a recovery that almost no level of crisis can surmount the barriers of class, race, party, and union affiliation that divide the state.

Chapter 8
THE POLICY CHOICES

Though many of the forces that will shape Michigan's future are beyond its control, the state has much more power to mold its own destiny than many recognize. If, over the next twenty years, the center of U.S. auto production gradually shifts away from Michigan, if Michigan firms do not capture a major share of the coming wave of manufacturing automation, or if Detroit continues to decline until it is no longer a major American city, it will not be an accident of history. It will be largely because of decisions taken and not taken in Michigan.

Over many years, the great wealth created by the automobile industry in Michigan has created an atmosphere of both complacency and partisanship within the state. Just as the nation spent most of the postwar era debating issues of equity and fairness, Michigan has grown accustomed to heated arguments over the distribution of the tax burden, the division of revenues between wages and profits, and the rights of poor and disadvantaged people. These issues were not wrong for the times, and they are still important today. But the next two decades will demand far more attention to the questions of efficiency and competitiveness, and to collective efforts to realize these objectives. Old habits of thinking and traditional relationships must change, particularly those built around adversarial positions and protection of long-standing rights.

Virtually all of the institutions in Michigan face the same challenge: to find politically acceptable ways in which to agree on shared future objectives and to make the changes needed to realize them. In many cases, the changes are so threatening that they cannot be achieved by the existing leadership or perhaps even by the existing institutions. But if changes are not negotiated, accepted, and implemented willingly, they will surely come anyway, sweeping aside the leaders and institutions that resist.

Complacency and inaction are the greatest risks. Three years ago, in the depths of a frightening recession, there was a widely shared sense of the need for change. Today, the return to normalcy is almost complete: both political parties are hurrying to cut taxes, Chrysler's workers are back to parity, and most of the laid-off auto workers have returned to work. If Michigan fails to come to terms with the need for major changes in policies and attitudes, the state can expect painful, unplanned changes to be forced upon it during the recessions that will inevitably occur over the next two decades.

What changes are needed? What are the choices that Michigan can make to increase its chances of prospering economically and socially over the next two decades? The greatest opportunities lie in four areas:

A. Regaining the Advantage as a Manufacturer of Automobiles

Two decades ago there was no doubt that Michigan was the most efficient place in the world to make cars. Today, Michigan is not only a more costly production location than Japan, it is apparently not the lowest cost site in the United States for new facilites.

But though the Saturn decision and others made by Japanese producers in the past five years suggest that Michigan is no longer the cost leader, the decision by Mazda to build in Flat Rock suggests that the state is still potentially competitive. The first, and most important, task for Michigan policymakers is to reestablish Michigan as the lowest cost location for auto manufacturing in the United States.

This task is urgent, not only because automobile manufacturing is the mainstay of Michigan's economy. More importantly, the industry's evolution offers the best chance for the state to adapt to, and profit from, the rapid changes taking place in

THE POLICY CHOICES

the U.S. economy. By the year 2005, manufacturing automation will have transformed American industry, spawning a wide range of new products (home robots might be an example) and creating a more capital intensive manufacturing system in which a smaller share of workers are engaged in direct production. Even manufacturing jobs will involve service skills: marketing, finance, engineering, maintenance, distribution, and research. If Michigan is to participate in this future manufacturing economy as successfully as it has in the current one, it must first reclaim its title as America's most efficient producer of automobiles.

Before serious action can be taken to regain Michigan's competitive advantage, the citizens and policymakers of the state must recognize the seriousness of the problem. Virtually no one in Michigan doubts the importance of automobiles to the future of the state. Yet, when individual issues are debated, the impacts of state policies on state competitiveness are often short changed.

Though it is sensible to seek to diversify Michigan's economy, policy initiatives that divert attention and resources away from actions that could be taken to support the auto industry are shortsighted. Michigan cannot expect food processing, forest products, or any other non-automotive industry to have more than a trivial impact on the state's future over the next two decades. Without collective agreement that "what's good for GM (and Ford, Chrysler, Mazda, and their suppliers) is good for Michigan," a continuing series of small, individually inconsequential decisions or non-decisions will fail to restore Michigan's competitiveness as a producer of automobiles. What can Michigan do to regain its competitive position? Four steps are most important:

1. Readjust the Wage Structure to Reflect Competitive Realities.

The higher wages paid to workers in the automobile industry, and to other workers in Southeast Michigan, are at the heart of the problem of competitiveness for the state. Over the next twenty years, this wage premium will almost certainly disappear. Either wages will be brought into line as a result of union negotiations or automotive production will gradually relocate to lower wage firms in other parts of the country and the world. For Michigan, the challenge is to ensure that wage adjustments occur at home before automotive production is moved away.

The state also might try to take a more visible leadership role in labor negotiations. Each time the UAW and the auto industry reach a national agreement governing wages and work rules, the consequences for Michigan are enormous. When negotiations take place, state leaders should not be shy about articulating the broad interests of all state residents, in addition to the narrower goals of auto workers and companies.

This is not a strategy of "getting poor." It does not mean that workers in Michigan must accept wages equal to those in Taiwan or Korea. It means simply that the state must manage its way back to wage parity with the rest of the nation or it will lose its status as the main producer of automobiles in the United States.

Although most of the decisions that can affect Michigan's wage structure are in the hands of union and management leaders, the state government can help the adjustment process. For example, as a potential partner with industry and labor in pursuing competitiveness, the state can seek to shoulder more of the costs (e.g., training) that are part of the current wage bill. To the extent that state policies have indirect impacts on the wage bill (for example, in the area of health care costs), efforts should be directed toward lowering these costs as much as possible. And in its own wage negotiations the state can seek to bring the salaries of its employees in line with those of other states, since these wages raise costs of living and working in the state.

2. Continue the Effort to Reduce Business Costs.

Over the past several years, state policymakers have vigorously debated issues such as workers' compensation, unemployment insurance, and business taxes. No matter what steps have been taken recently or what is done in the next few years, it is important to understand that these issues will not go away. The interstate competition for employment generating facilites will intensify over the next 20 years. Even though government-imposed business costs are not the most dominant elements of business location decisions, they are still important at the margin. Unless Michigan can completely reposition itself to be among the states with the lowest state-imposed business costs, there will be continuous pressure to address and readdress these program and tax issues. Because Michigan no longer holds a natural competitive advantage, the objective must be to achieve below-average rates of business taxation, not just to bring the state back into line with other states (where, for example, it already stands in the area of non-wage business taxes). Obviously, these issues raise difficult and emotional issues of fairness and humanitarian needs, but state policymakers cannot afford to lose sight of the impacts of these programs on the competitiveness of its leading industry.

   3. Become a Full Partner with Labor and Management in the Drive for Competitiveness.

In its quest for the Saturn plant, Michigan proposed a far-reaching partnership with General Motors and the UAW. This program included a fresh approach to state regulatory policies, investment in site development and worker training, programs to develop the support base of suppliers, and other measures. This was a sensible and dynamic strategy for attracting the Saturn complex. Although the effort failed to attract the plant, this program, particularly its regulatory, training, and research components, should be implemented now on an industry-wide basis. Rather than shelving the initiative and returning to business as usual, Michigan should treat its continuing relationship with the auto industry with the same sense of urgency and eagerness that it devoted to the Saturn competition. The University of Michigan's Auto-In-Michigan project has recently suggested a number of concrete strategies for implementing this partnership; its recommendations deserve bipartisan consideration and support.

4. Increase of State Investments in Advanced Technologies and Engineering Eeucation.

Michigan has already made a substantial commitment to develop its high-technology research capabilities, particularly in the area of robotics. Because of the overriding importance of these technologies to the future health of the auto industry, and to the development of 21st century industries in Michigan, the state should be willing to boost investments in these technologies far beyond what it has currently committed. The target areas should include not only robotics and computer-integrated manufacturing technologies, but also new materials development and fabrication, including especially engineering plastics and ceramics.

These technologies have, of course, already been identified as important to Michigan and many other states. The scale of investments does not yet match, however, the agreement on their importance. In early 1985, Michigan offered General Motors tax and spending incentives totaling approximately $660 million to locate a single plant in the state. The development of a larger base of research and technology to support the auto industry is at least as important, and has returns that are at least as great as those projected from the Saturn facility. It is not unreasonable to suggest that resources on the Saturn scale should be directed toward building the base of technological and educational infrastructure from which the high-tech auto and related industries will grow.

Michigan should systematically seek to attract the leading educators and the most talented students in these areas. The state already has an outstanding reputation and capabilities in several of the areas. The goal now should be to ensure that key Michigan universities offer not just equivalent but superior salaries, facilities, fellowships, equipment, and consulting opportunities to outstanding professionals and students in the

THE POLICY CHOICES

In order to succeed with such a strategy, the state should recognize that it cannot afford to attract the best and brightest in every discipline, nor can it bolster the research capabilities of many of its universities. Even though Michigan has substantial resources, it should not try compete for scholars across the board as, for example, the University of Texas has recently attempted. Instead, the state should concentrate on automotive-related technologies (a relatively broad field in any case), where it already has substantial resources and advantages.

B. Delivering Government Services More Efficiently: Setting New Priorities and Privatizing the Bureaucracy

Of the Michigan institutions that must change to meet the realities of the 1990s and beyond, state government has the most difficult challenge. Though the state's political leaders usually respond quickly to the voters, they are often unable to forge a consensus for change when its consequences are painful for many of the electorate. More importantly, the large bureaucracies that deliver state and local services tend to be generally inflexible. Unlike the managers and employees of private companies who must sometimes accept unwelcome changes in pay and organization in order to survive in the market, no market imposes change upon most government institutions. As a result, government is often the last to adjust to new realities, especially when they threaten the interests of large groups of employees.

Over the next twenty years government in Michigan will face constant pressure to deliver its services with greater efficiency. With a work force that is well paid relative to other states, with less federal aid and unchecked demands for new government services, with slower growth of population, and a declining ability of the auto industry to generate new jobs at premium wages, the squeeze in Michigan is likely to be severe.

One approach to this pressure is simply to seek across-the-board cuts in state and local spending, mirroring proposals currently under consideration at the federal level. Those who view all government expenditures as a misallocation of resources believe such a strategy offers the best chance of curbing government waste.

Such an approach is likely to be short-sighted. While it is sensible to be skeptical of unchecked government spending, government performs many essential social and economic services. Michigan's success over the next two decades, measured in terms of its economic development and the quality of the lives of its residents, depends to a great degree on the type and quality of the services delivered by state and local government. Short of a "withering away" of government, the state must find a way to provide more with less.

Two basic strategies deserve consideration:

1. *Experiment With Privatization of Public Services*

The decision to use tax dollars to support public services has typically been taken as the signal to create government bureaucracies to deliver those services. For most services, this is not necessary. An increasing number of state and local governments are beginning to experiment with a wide variety of contracting arrangements for the delivery of government services.

For example, a 1982 study by the U.S. Department of Housing and Urban Development showed that a third of all U.S. cities contracted at least one public service, including sanitation, fire protection, and park maintenance services at the local level, as well as operation of prisons, mass transit systems, schools, and public health clinics. By mid-1984, twenty-seven cities had hired private contractors to provide bus and van services; a dozen jurisdictions had opted for private detention facilities; more than fifteen were using private fire departments.

The results of these experiments have often been highly favorable, with typical savings reported as ranging from 10 percent to more than 50 percent. Private entrepreneurs often find efficiencies in the use of workers, newer or better capital

THE POLICY CHOICES

equipment, economies of scale, less restrictive work rules, or lower wage scales.

Of course, privatization of public services is not without risks. It requires a bureaucracy to administer, audit, and manage the contractors. The opportunities for collusion, bid-rigging, and corruption are always present. Efforts to ensure the fairness of the competitive bidding process often lead to cumbersome and costly paperwork requirements that undermine the hoped-for savings. And the creation of a new group of private entities with a vested interest in increased public spending can create great pressure to boost government outlays.

But, despite these potential drawbacks, the benefits of contracting outweigh the costs. By bringing the discipline of the market to bear on public services, the system provides automatic correction for the rigidities in wages, work rules, and benefit structures that creep into government institutions. Not only can contractors often perform given jobs better and more cheaply, the challenge of competition often leads to rapid improvements in the efficiency and cost-effectiveness of the public bureaucracy. Thus, even an experimental program can have far-reaching impacts on the cost and quality of government services.

Despite the obvious political difficulties of contracting out public services in Michigan, the state has much to gain from such a program. Just as the automobile industry has turned to new relationships with suppliers and subsidiaries as a way of breaking free of its accumulated corporate fat, the governments in Michigan will benefit from a similar shakeup of institutional relationships. Equally importantly, such a program would measurably enhance national perceptions of the state among the press, public, and financial communities, repositioning it as a leader in innovation, and a proponent, rather than an opponent, of change.

Virtually no system or program in the state should be immune from consideration. Several obvious possibilities include the operation of the correctional system, the administration of state-funded health programs, and management of state welfare and unemployment insurance programs.

At the local level, the opportunities are even greater. Not only traditional candidates such as trash collection, but unconventional ones such as fire and even police services, might potentially be contracted. Even sacrosanct services such as education might be more effectively delivered in some cases by private contractors. For example, in school districts where discipline, test scores, and the general quality of education have been criticized by parents and public officials, privatization offers an alternative that carries few risks compared to the current program. A contractor prepared to commit to specific educational goals, with profits pegged to performance, might be able to achieve educational progress where current systems have failed.

Contracting for public services need not involve any loss of public control. On the contrary, properly structured contracts which set performance standards and monitor contractor progress are likely to make these public services *more* responsive to public wishes, as well as cheaper and more efficient.

2. *Adopt an Investment Strategy to Reallocate State Spending*

While the categories are not exact, state government spending may be roughly allocated into two broad categories: programs that support current consumption, such as income support and public services, and programs with long-term returns, such as highways, economic development and education. Over the past 15 years, Michigan's spending has been increasingly biased toward consumption rather than investment. For example, Michigan spent 95 percent more per capita on welfare than the average for all other states in 1983, and its welfare spending has grown almost twice as fast since 1970 as the national average. By contrast, Michigan's education spending, which was 32 percent above the national average in 1970, was only 10 percent above the norm in 1983. In 1983 its highway spending was 14 percent below the regional average, and 32 below the national average.

THE POLICY CHOICES

These priorities should be reversed. To succeed in the competitive environment of the future, Michigan should systematically realign its priorities to favor spending that will accelerate economic growth and generate wealth over the long term. In budgetary terms, Michigan should try to think of itself more as Michigan, Inc., a sophisticated corporation that is constantly reinvesting its profits in research, personnel development, new products and advanced technologies. Specifically, Michigan's capital programs in the areas of higher education, transportation, economic development, advanced training and industry development deserve higher priority, while those aimed at providing social and public services, and income transfers deserve more careful scrutiny.

Within favored program categories, more attention needs to be given to the returns from the investments made. For example, whatever the ultimate success of the Detroit People Mover, it is indisputable that the money could have been better spent on other transportation needs in Detroit and elsewhere in the state. Similarly, investments by the Land Trust in new state acreage appear to be some of the least productive ways to invest state resources for long-term gains.

The need for such a budgetary realignment is made especially important because of the trends in federal spending. As the Detroit People Mover illustrated, Michigan spending has been directed to a great degree by federal dictates and priorities. It would never have been attempted had the money for it been available to the state without restrictions.

Now Michigan may find its priorities being similarly skewed by federal cutbacks. To date, the major reductions in federal programs have been concentrated in the social spending programs initiated during the 1960s and 1970s. If Michigan simply tries to "pick up the slack" by replacing the federal dollars for these programs with state and local funding, its budgets are likely to be increasingly directed toward consumption rather than investment spending. Instead, the state should consciously seek to set its priorities according to a long term strategy for growth. Without such a plan, investment spending is certain to be slighted during the periodic economic recessions that lie ahead.

C. Attracting People in Michigan

In the 1950s, when Gallup asked Americans where they "might like to move," Michigan was not among the top ten most attractive states, ranking not only behind such favorites as California, Arizona, and Colorado, but also behind midwestern rivals such as Illinois and Ohio. Yet throughout the 1950s and 1960s, the state grew faster than the rest of the nation and faster than Illinois and Ohio, because of the powerful economic pull of the automobile industry.

Over the next two decades, the auto industry will be unable to provide the same stimulus for population growth. At the same time, an increasing number of individuals (and businesses) will have ever-greater freedom to act on their preferences concerning where they want to live. Retirees and college students, and many professionals, can live almost wherever they wish. Unless the state can succeed in creating and marketing a quality of life that is at least as attractive as that of other states, it is likely to grow less quickly than other parts of the country.

Because the growth of most service industries is directly dependent on population (e.g., retailing, health care, education, finance), a stagnant or dwindling population has potentially negative consequences. By making Michigan a less attractive site for service industry investment, population losses could become a self-perpetuating spiral, just as population growth can be a self-generating economic stimulus.

Michigan has many advantages in the competition for people. It already has a large population base, and the universities, cultural centers, and sports arenas that have grown up to serve these people. It has scenic areas, particularly along its thousands of miles of lake frontage, that are unmatched in the Midwest. And though its climate is not the equal of

THE POLICY CHOICES

California's, many Americans find Michigan's four seasons far more attractive than those of, for example, Texas or Georgia.

In order better to exploit its natural advantages, Michigan should more consciously seek to attract and hold those people with the greatest choice of where to live: college students, young professionals, and retirees. In addition, the state should focus more attention on developing the facilities needed to attract tourists to the state.

Because the state's population will be gradually aging over the next 20 years, and because the auto industry is likely to use retirement as one of the main mechanisms for shrinking its labor force, the state has a particularly great interest in enhancing its status as a retirement center. Whether the large number of pension and social security checks due to auto industry retirees are mailed to addresses in Tucson or Traverse City will have a great impact on the economic health of the state over the next 20 years.

What can be done? Beyond the general, widely-agreed on policies, such as maintaining strong environmental regulations and preserving the state's clean water resources, the state should tailor aggressive efforts to attract desirable residents. For example:

*1. Promoting Michigan as a Vacation and
Retirement Community*

Michigan has identified tourism promotion as a priority. Yet the meager resources devoted to the "Say Yes to Michigan" campaign belie the real importance of this objective. If Michigan is truly serious about making the state a vacation and retirement mecca, it should be willing to make a concerted effort to promote development of the attractive lake country areas in the Northern lower peninsula. For example, state spending for highways and airports serving these areas might be retargeted to better promote growth. Spending for parks and recreation should be given a far greater priority than its current status as an afterthought to the state budget. State and local policies that restrict development should be reevaluated. Economic development spending, which has been heavily skewed toward attracting heavy industry, could be redirected. Advertising spending might be increased. Taxes that discourage visitors (e.g., levies on hotel rooms), or that make it expensive to die in Michigan (inheritance taxes), could be reduced. If Michigan is to become the leading tourist destination in the Midwest, it must bend all of its policies to the task.

2. *Attracting and Keeping Young Professionals*

People in their early twenties have the greatest freedom to choose where they wish to live. When picking a college or seeking a first job, young people often have a much wider range of options than later in their lives, when jobs, mortgages, and friends will tie them to their current communities. The state can do more to make it easy to "Choose Michigan." For example, college tuition, for both in and out-of-state residents, is usually debated in the context of budgets and ability to pay. But as the California system has demonstrated, cheap, high-quality higher education can be a tool for encouraging people to move to the state. And the experience of several years of living and learning in the state can make these students more willing to settle or return to Michigan in later years.

Of course, the greatest incentive for young people to move to or stay in Michigan is economic: available and well-paying jobs. But, in addition to efforts to support healthy auto and auto-related industries, the state may be able to
increase the attractiveness of jobs for young people in Michigan. For example, a program of low interest mortgages for first-time home buyers, funded by government, union, and corporate pension funds, and not restricted to certain areas, as previous programs have been, could increase the economic pull of job offers in Michigan. While such incentives should be evaluated with care, they might prove to be at least as effective in supporting Michigan employers as industrial revenue bonds or business tax abatements.

THE POLICY CHOICES

D. Adopting Metropolitan Policies for Michigan's Cities

If Michigan is to be able to attract people who have many choices open to them, cities across the state must be able to provide culture, diversity, and excitement, as well as jobs and homes. The ability of many cities to supply these values has been compromised by artificial political boundaries. For example, looked at as a region, the Detroit metropolitan area offers a wide range of amenities and tremendous vitality. It is only when Detroit is defined only as the city south of Eight Mile Road that the picture is one of deterioration and despair.

All of Detroit's severe economic and social problems are exacerbated by its geographic limits. The fiscal bind that the city faces, the deep divisions between races, and the political antipathies that dominate regional discussions are all rooted in the jurisdictional separation of the city and its suburbs. If Detroit's political boundaries matched the real boundaries of urban development in Southeast Michigan, the city's perception of itself, and the nation's perception of Michigan, would be radically different.

Of course, it would not be easy politically to redraw political boundaries in Southeast Michigan (although it may be more feasible elsewhere in the state). But from the state's point of view, the objective should be to see that Detroit and other Michigan cities--seen as metropolitan regions rather than as the currently defined jurisdictions--are self-sustaining, growing urban centers. Rather than treating the cities as expensive problems, the state should design its policies to encourage regional decisionmakers to focus on shared opportunities and collective responsibilities.

In practice, this may mean that the state tries to develop more institutions for regional cooperation, such as SEMTA or Detroit's regional water system. It might mean encouragement of collaboration between local jurisdictions to provide shared services where there are significant economies of scale or other efficiencies to be gained. In some areas, it might mean action to promote annexation or mergers. In others, it could involve imposition of shared sales or local income taxes to equalize revenue bases.

All of these steps, of course, arouse the most heated debates and antipathies, particularly in Southeast Michigan, because they so often threaten established powers and organizations. In each case, the form that metropolitan policies take will be different, with a delicate political and economic calculus necessary to accomplish anything. But the state must find ways to escape from the trap that rigid local boundaries have imposed on future urban development and response to change.

E. Agreeing on a Shared Agenda For Action

To many readers, these policy suggestions will seem either too conventional (invest in new automotive technologies) or too impolitic (privatize public services) to be useful. Others will dismiss them as part of a partisan agenda, despite the degree to which they parallel suggestions made in the "Path to Prosperity."

Many, who are accustomed to thinking of Michigan as the state where millions labor at bending metal and other honest (if boring) work, will revolt at policies that are designed to
promote a Michigan filled with academics, salesmen, and retirees. Many who remember Michigan as the site of one of the great advances in American social justice--the wage bargain that finally conferred middle class status on average working people--will see any call for lower wages as a betrayal of fundamental principles. Many who see themselves primarily through the lens of their race, class, or party will be unable to agree that there is more to gain by compromise than by confrontation.

But regardless of how these policies are evaluated, the state of Michigan has an overriding interest in debating and deciding on a strategy for the future. Even where there has been broad agreement on goals, partisanship and mistrust have made it difficult for the state to respond to change.

THE POLICY CHOICES

Continued failure to agree on the need for change, and failure to set a course of action, will leave Michigan's future largely in the hands of decisionmakers in Tokyo, Washington, or other state capitals. Debate, followed by action, will allow Michigan to shape its own future.

882571

HC
107
.M5
J64
1987

HC107.M5J64 1987
Johnston, William B., 1945-
Michigan beyond 2000 /

BAKER COLLEGE LIBRARY

3 3504 00097 4545

HC
107
.M5
J64
1987

Johnston, William B., 1945-

Michigan beyond 2000

DATE DUE

PROPERTY OF
BAKER COLLEGE
Owosso Campus